CAN'T HANG OUT...
GOTTA
BUILD A SHIP

CAN'T HANG OUT...
GOTTA BUILD A SHIP

SHANE BARKER

CFI
AN IMPRINT OF CEDAR FORT, INC.
SPRINGVILLE, UTAH

This is a work of fiction. The characters, names, incidents, places, and dialogue are products of the author's imagination and are not to be construed as real. The views expressed within this work are the sole responsibility of the author and do not necessarily reflect the position of Cedar Fort, Inc., or any other entity.

ISBN 13: 978-1-4621-1030-8

Published by CFI, an imprint of Cedar Fort, Inc.
2373 W. 700 S., Springville, UT, 84663
Distributed by Cedar Fort, Inc., www.cedarfort.com

LIBRARY OF CONGRESS CATALOGING-IN-PUBLICATION DATA

Barker, Shane R., author.
  Can't hang out--gotta build a ship : unleashing your inner Nephi / Shane Barker.
    pages cm
  Summary: Focuses on topics like dealing with siblings, setbacks, disappointments, and adversity by using Nephi (from the Book of Mormon) as an example of how to cope.
  ISBN 978-1-4621-1030-8 (alk. paper)
  1. Mormon youth--Conduct of life. 2. Nephi (Book of Mormon figure) I. Title.

  BX8643.Y6B355 2012
  248.8'30882893--dc23

                        2012010788

Cover and page design by Danie Romrell
Cover design © 2012 by Lyle Mortimer
Edited by Kelley Konzak

Printed in the United States of America

10 9 8 7 6 5 4 3 2 1

Printed on acid-free paper.

FOR BEN, CHRISTIAN, JORDAN, AND STEVE

TABLE OF CONTENTS

ONE ⊙ THE SANTA CLAUS THING
UNLEASHING YOUR INNER NEPHI

"Okay, hotshots . . . try this one."

I uncapped a marker and wrote

$$3(2x+4) + 5(3x+6)$$

on the classroom whiteboard.

I turned and looked out at my class.

"Can anyone tell me what to do first?"

I was expecting someone to say, "Distribute the three!" or maybe, "Use the distributive property!" So I was totally unprepared to hear a seventh-grade boy named Jake yell out, "You do the Santa Claus thing!"

The class went silent while everyone turned to look at Jake. He was the undisputed clown of the class, and it wasn't unusual to hear him say something silly.

But "the Santa Claus thing"?

Jake's response was so ridiculous that even his friends were pulling faces as if wondering *What in the world are you talking about?*

But Jake was grinning happily. "Am I right?"

"The Santa Claus thing?" I shook my head. "I have no idea what you're talking about."

"Look," he said, getting up from his desk and walking to the

1

front of the room. He took my marker and said, "First you draw the lines . . ."

He quickly sketched arcs over the problem like this:

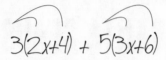

"And then"—He turned to look out at the class as if divulging a great secret—"you turn them into Santa Claus hats."

He quickly finished his sketch:

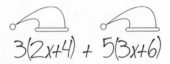

The class howled.

I shook my head as Jake strutted back to his desk. It was fun to see the class having a good time, but I knew I'd never again mention the distributive property without someone calling it "the Santa Claus thing."

The class remained riled for a moment (Jake's friends were all punching him and tussling his hair), but then a young woman named Ellen raised her hand.

"Yes, Ellen?"

She scrunched her nose as if embarrassed. "Can I ask you a question?"

"Of course you can."

"Promise you won't get mad?"

"Do I *ever* get mad?"

Jake's eyes went as wide as pepperoni pizzas, but before he could voice his opinion, I said, "I promise I won't get mad. What's your question?"

"Why do we have to learn this?"

The class went instantly silent again.

I sighed. Because I'm a junior high math teacher, I hear that question all the time. And I've always hated it. Most of the students who ask it are just unhappy about having to do a little work. But Ellen sounded sincere. And even Jake was watching me intently.

"All right," I said. "You want the long answer or the short one?"

"Short, I guess."

"Okay. Can you tell me which math classes we teach in this school?"

"Pre-algebra!" someone shouted.

"Pre-algebra," I agreed. "That's what we're learning here. What else?"

"Algebra!"

"Geometry!"

"Algebra two!"

"Terminometry!" (That was Jake.)

"It's called *trigonometry*, Jake. But we don't teach it in junior high."

I walked to the middle of the room, where I was closer to the kids. "I teach all of those classes, so I know what you're going to learn in them. But more important, I know what you *need to know* to succeed in them."

I pointed at the problem on the board. "That Santa Claus thing? You'll need to know how to do that next year in algebra. You'll need to know it in geometry and in algebra two."

I turned back to Ellen. "And that's why I'm teaching it to you. The better you learn it now, the easier algebra will be for you next year. And the better you'll understand it."

It was a simple answer, but Ellen was nodding. So were many of the other kids. (Even Jake was looking at his Santa Claus hats a little more tolerantly.)

I probably wouldn't have thought any more about that. But during priesthood meeting that Sunday, the deacons quorum was talking about the Book of Mormon.

"The Nephites never read the Book of Mormon," our advisor,

Brother Shurtz, said. "It was written for *us*. Mormon saw our day, and he knew the challenges we'd face. So when he abridged the records, he included those stories, sermons, and events he knew would most help *us*."

Brother Shurtz took a moment to look at each of the boys in the quorum. "So when you read the Book of Mormon, you have to keep asking yourself, 'Why did Mormon include *this* story?' or 'Why did he include *that* lesson?' You have to figure out why it's important to *you*."

President Ezra Taft Benson once said: "The Book of Mormon was written for us today. It is a record of a fallen people, compiled by inspired men for our blessing today. Those people never had the book—it was meant for us. Mormon, the ancient prophet after whom the book is named, abridged centuries of records. God, who knows the end from the beginning, told him what to include in his abridgement that we would need for our day" ("The Book of Mormon Is the Word of God," *Ensign*, May 1975, 63).

I'm not sure what the boys thought of that. But my mind was reeling. I was suddenly looking at the Book of Mormon in a whole new light. It wasn't just an ancient record about ancient people.

It was written for *me*.

And it was written for *you*. Mormon included the thoughts and ideas he knew would help *us* deal with the trials and challenges we face every day.

I was watching the Winter Olympics once on TV. The downhill ski course was especially steep, tricky, and treacherous, and because of a wild snowstorm, the racers weren't able to ski it before the race. They weren't able to inspect the sharp curves, steep drops, and hairpin turns they'd encounter as they blazed down the hill at full speed.

So they went to Plan B.

As soon as each racer finished their run, they grabbed a phone and called their teammates back up the mountain. They described the course in detail, warning their teammates of problems and dangers. They told them where the tricky parts were. They gave

I was once driving through a mountain canyon late at night. As I approached a series of sharp curves, an approaching car began flashing its lights at me. The next car to drive around the bend did the same thing.

What's going on? I wondered.

I slowed down and, as I rounded the bend, saw a huge herd of elk crossing the road. There must have been thirty or forty animals, many of them standing right in the middle of the road. I was driving slow enough that I was able to stop without hitting any of them.

But if I hadn't been warned—if I hadn't slowed down—I would have plowed right into them.

I was grateful that someone who had seen the road ahead had warned me of the danger.

Mormon, Moroni, and others have seen the road ahead of us, giving us tips, suggestions, and warnings to help us through tough times.

them suggestions for skiing the course as fast and safely as possible.

The result was that their teammates knew what to expect. They knew what dangers to look for. They knew what hazards to avoid. They knew how to attack the course in order to ski their best race.

In a real way, that's what ancient prophets have done for us. Nephi, Mormon, and Moroni all saw our day. They *knew* and they *saw* the challenges and dangers *we* would face. And then they gave us tips, ideas, and suggestions to guide us through them. They gave us examples and stories from their own lives to help us live the best life we can.

Take Nephi, for instance.

I love what it says in the Book of Mormon Student Study Guide: "Nephi was . . . a scholar, a great hunter, a blacksmith, a shipbuilder, a navigator, a goldsmith, a record keeper, a refugee, a temple builder, a king, a warrior, a prophet, and a seer. Do you think a man with that kind of experience could teach us something about life?" (Book of Mormon Student Study Guide (2000), 13).

Ya think?

Remember that the Lord taught Nephi how to build a ship; he can help you with your science project.

He taught Nephi the meaning of Lehi's dream; he can help you understand algebra.

He helped Nephi obtain the plates of brass; he can help you accomplish your assignments, projects, and callings.

The Lord teamed up with Nephi again and again and again, helping him through rough times. He will be there when you need him too.

Nephi had experiences that can help *you* in your life. *Today.* You can take his experiences and apply them *today* to whatever challenges you're facing in school, in your family, with your friends, and in every other aspect of your life.

Having trouble with your brothers or sisters?

Nephi's felt your pain.

Trouble at school?

Nephi has a few insights.

Building your testimony?

Oh, yeah . . . Nephi has a few thoughts on that.

And you see, that's what this book is about. It's about taking Nephi's experiences and applying them to *your* life. It's about taking the lessons Nephi learned and using them to make your own life better, happier, and more successful.

Let me give you an example.

When I was in college, I had a bad experience with one of my teachers. The details aren't important, but I felt like he'd treated me unfairly. And that made me mad.

But I'll show him! I thought. *Yeah . . . I'll teach him not to mess with me!*

What did I do?

Probably the most un-Nephi-like thing in the world: I quit working.

I quit trying.

I kept thinking, *You're really gonna treat me like that? Well, I'll show you! I'll just fail this class!*

Yeah, yeah, I know . . . I was being stupid. And immature. If Nephi had been there, he would have taken Laban's sword and smacked me over the head with it.

I once spent the summer running the rifle range at a Boy Scout camp. But with less than a week until camp was to open, our rifles hadn't been delivered.

Well, this is great, I thought. *Trying to run a rifle range without rifles. I might as well try teaching canoeing without canoes. Or teach swimming without a lake.*

But Nephi . . . he was unstoppable. I knew that in my place he would have found a way to get the job done. And I decided that I was going to be like Nephi.

I knew that Nephi wouldn't give up, so I decided that I wasn't going to give up either.

I called the sporting goods store we bought our supplies from and asked the gunsmith if he had any suggestions. He hemmed and hawed for a couple of minutes, then said, "Let me call you back."

Two days later, a delivery truck came roaring into camp. And then another. And another. And another.

The gunsmith had called every sporting goods store in the county, scrounging up enough rifles that we were able to start the summer off with a bang!

It would have been easy to have just given up. But Nephi had taught me what it meant to be unstoppable. He had given me an awesome example to follow.

And that example made all the difference.

But I was sitting in my Book of Mormon class one day and happened to read 2 Nephi 1:23: "Awake, my sons; put on the armor of righteousness. Shake off the chains with which ye are bound, and come forth out of obscurity, and arise from the dust."

Ouch!

"Shake off the chains with which ye are bound."

Those words hit me like a ton of bricks. I felt like Lehi was speaking directly to me, saying, "Hey! You're *better* than this! Grow up! Quit acting like a little kid and get over it! You're not hurting anyone but yourself, and if you don't shape up, you're going to regret it!"

I felt so embarrassed that I actually looked around the room to see if anyone was watching.

But it wasn't over. I flipped over a couple of pages and read, "Wherefore, ye must press *forward* with a steadfastness in Christ, having a perfect brightness of hope, and a love of God and of all men. Wherefore, if ye shall press *forward*, feasting upon the word of Christ, and endure to the end, behold, thus saith the Father: Ye shall have eternal life" (2 Nephi 31:20, emphasis added).

In the margin beside that verse, I'd written, "Stop looking back at things that are behind you! The Lord put our eyes in the front of our head for a reason: we're supposed to look *forward*, not backward!"

Once again, I felt like an ancient prophet was speaking right to me, telling me to quit worrying about dumb things and to start looking ahead. And Nephi's words couldn't have hit me any harder if the Angel Moroni had dropped the golden plates on top of me.

Yeah, I changed my attitude.

I cleaned up my act.

I apologized to my teacher and got back to work.

Not only did I end up earning an A in the class, but my teacher actually went out of his way to help me earn an internship as an editor in the Church Office Building.

Later on I remember thinking, *Thank you, Lehi, for your counsel.*

Thank you, Nephi, for yours.

And thank you, Mormon, for knowing those lessons would help me . . . and for including them in your book.

Now how does any of that apply to you?

Okay.

Remember when Nephi and his brothers returned to Jerusalem for the plates of brass? Let me give you a quick refresher:

NEPHI RETURNS TO JERUSALEM!

Lehi asks Nephi and his brothers to return to Jerusalem to get the plates of brass from Laban. This is a round trip of about 360 miles and will take nearly a month, but Nephi immediately says yes. He *knows* that the Lord will provide a way to get the job done.

The Lord helps Nephi to convince Laban's servant Zoram that he (Nephi) is actually Laban. Zoram gives Nephi the plates.

The brothers politely ask Laban for the plates, but he becomes angry and chases them out of the city.

The Lord delivers Laban into Nephi's hand.

The brothers try buying the plates with the gold, silver, and other precious things they left behind when they went into the wilderness. Laban takes their property and sends his servants to slay them.

Laman and Lemuel want to give up, but Nephi is determined to get the job done. Even though he knows Laban's men will kill him if they catch him, he sneaks back into the city, knowing that the Lord will provide a way for him to get the plates.

9

Wow!

What an awesome adventure!

But have you ever wondered why Mormon included it? After all, it's more than just a rattling good adventure.

Imagine for a moment that you were able to talk with Nephi for a couple of minutes . . . and imagine that you could ask him anything you wanted.

Anything!

Wouldn't that be cool?

Imagine being able to say, "Nephi . . . I'm really having a tough time in school. I'm just not getting it! What do you think I should do?"

Or maybe you'd say, "Nephi, I'm trying my best to be good! I really am! But it's just so *tough* sometimes . . . What do you think I should do?"

Wouldn't that be awesome?

Wouldn't it be fun to hear what he'd say?

We'll probably never have the chance to actually ask him anything face-to-face (at least in this life). And Nephi knew that. So he shared thoughts and experiences that—if we *read* them and *ponder* them—might still give us those answers we're looking for.

Let's take another look at Nephi's adventure with the brass plates, and I'll show you what I mean.

When Lehi asked his sons to return to Jerusalem, Nephi didn't complain. He didn't whine, he didn't moan, and he didn't make excuses. He immediately said, "*Yes.*"

Suppose your parents ask you to do something. Suppose your bishop or Young Women leader gives you a tough project or assignment. What would Nephi encourage you to do?

Nephi didn't just agree to get the job done; he also did it with a *good attitude*.

When your parents (or Church leaders) ask you to do something, what sort of attitude should *you* have?

Nephi and his brothers tried twice to get the plates but failed both times. Laman and Lemuel both wanted to give up and go home, but Nephi refused to quit. He wasn't going to let *anything* stop him from getting the job done.

Suppose you're having trouble with a job or chore of your own. Maybe you're having a tough time in school, struggling with biology or French. Or maybe you're just feeling discouraged, having a tough time with your part-time job, club, or ball team. If you had a chance to ask Nephi for advice, what do you think he'd tell you?

Even though Laban's men were out hunting for him with orders to kill, Nephi went back into the city a third time. He didn't know what he was going to do, but he had faith that the Lord would provide a solution.

Imagine being given a job or assignment that seems impossible to you. What do you suppose Nephi would say about that?

Nephi's brothers were a pain to work with. They whined, complained, nagged, and stirred things up again and again and *again*. But Nephi never gave up on them. He not only put up with their antics but also constantly tried to encourage them, motivate them, and inspire them to be better.

I'm certain that your brothers and sisters are all as easy to get along with as you are. But when things *do* get a little tense, how would Nephi suggest you handle things?

No, Laman and Lemuel weren't the best brothers. But no matter what they did, no matter how rotten they were, Nephi forgave them *every single time*!

Okay, this might hurt a little bit . . . but if your brothers or sisters ever do something that upsets you, *what would Nephi suggest that you do?*

When Nephi found Laban drunk in the street, the Spirit constrained Nephi to slay him. Nephi didn't want to do that! He'd never killed anyone before. But he trusted his Father in Heaven and he *was* obedient.

You too might be given counsel that you don't like. You may not want to wait until you're sixteen to date. You may not see anything wrong with playing a little ball on the Sabbath. You may not see any harm in piercing your tongue or getting a flashy tattoo.

But what does Nephi's example tell you about listening to Church leaders?

Okay! See how it works? In that one simple story are all *kinds* of lessons we can learn. There are all kinds of ways to apply Nephi's experiences to our own. There are all kinds of tips for blessing and enriching our lives, bringing us closer to our Father in Heaven.

Which is exactly why they're there!

This is a *fun* book! It was fun to write, and I think you'll find it fun to read.

So let's jump right in!

Let's get to work!

Start today. Unleash your "inner Nephi" and transform your life into a fantastic, uplifting adventure!

THERE ARE A LOT OF WAYS NEPHI'S EXAMPLE CAN HELP US TODAY.

When I was once going through a tough time, I tried looking up different ways Nephi used to deal with discouragement.

Here are a few of my favorites:

- He read his scriptures (2 Nephi 4:15).

- He pondered the scriptures he read, maybe thinking of ways to apply them to his situation (2 Nephi 4:16).

- He remained faithful, trusting his Heavenly Father to help him through the tough times (2 Nephi 4:20–21, 34).

- He went to his Heavenly Father in "mighty prayer" (2 Nephi 4:24).

- He kept himself busy, working hard and being "industrious" (2 Nephi 5:15, 17).

- He kept a good attitude, knowing there were reasons for those tough times (1 Nephi 18:11).

- He counted his blessings, focusing on all the things going right in his life instead of the things going wrong (1 Nephi 18:16).

MY FRIEND ETHAN ONCE GAVE A TALK ON HOW NEPHI

might have stacked up as a Boy Scout. Following the Scout Law, his ideas went something like this:

- **Trustworthy:** Whether it was getting the brass plates, obtaining food for the family, or building a ship, you could always count on Nephi to get the job done.

- **Loyal:** Nephi was loyal to his parents, supporting them even when times were tough. And he was loyal to his Heavenly Father, living the commandments and being obedient at all times.

- **Helpful:** Nephi taught his brothers the gospel. He also hunted, doing his share of chores by finding food for the family.

- **Friendly:** Nephi was respectful to his mother, and he set a good example to his brothers. (He especially seemed to watch over his younger brothers Jacob and Joseph.) Don't you think he was friendly?

- **Courteous:** I believe Nephi showed great respect for his mother. He honors his parents in the very first sentence of the Book of Mormon.

- **Kind:** No matter how rotten they were to him, Nephi was always quick to forgive his brothers. (I bet he was Jacob and Joseph's favorite brother.)

- **Obedient:** When the Lord asked him to do something, Nephi didn't argue, he didn't question, he didn't complain, and he didn't check the calendar to see if he had the time. He said yes, and he then went right to work.

- **Cheerful:** Nephi always looked on the bright side of things. When he was tied up in the bottom of the ship—and later when he lost his father, Lehi—Nephi counted his blessings, focusing on those things going right for him rather than dwelling on his problems.

- **Thrifty:** Nephi possessed a bow made out of fine steel. And I think he took care of it, seeing as it lasted longer than Laman's or Lemuel's.

- **Brave:** Nephi snuck into Jerusalem, knowing that Laban's servants would kill him if they caught him. And then he actually dared to sneak right into Laban's house! (And he certainly wasn't afraid to stand up to his older brothers.)

- **Clean:** Nephi was honest, true, chaste, benevolent, virtuous . . . of course he was clean!

- **Reverent:** Nephi cared about sacred things. And he counseled his older brothers about the irreverent way they were acting aboard the ship while they were on the Lord's errand.

TWO ⦿⦿⦿ I GOTTA GET A DATE!
DEALING WITH SIBLINGS

"Girls!"

Sixteen-year-old Ammon Woolley trudged into the kitchen and slumped into a chair.

"I'm totally giving up on girls," he announced. "I mean it. I'm never asking another girl out in my life!"

Ammon's older sister Emily looked up from her homework.

"Why?" she asked. "What happened?"

"Britney just called me," Ammon said. "You know, the girl I was taking to the team barbecue tonight?" He shook his head. "Her family is in St. George, and they decided to spend an extra night, so she can't go now."

"Big deal," Emily said. "Just call someone else."

Ammon looked over with his best I-wish-it-was-that-easy expression.

"Riiiight," he said. "What am I supposed to say? 'Hi! I just got dumped, and since you couldn't *possibly* have any plans, I thought maybe you'd go out with me . . .'"

Emily was patient. "If you want to sit home and feel sorry for yourself, go ahead. But if you really want to go to the barbecue, get on the phone and *call someone*!"

"How long have you known me?" Ammon asked, holding his hands out. "It's hard enough for me to get dates a month in advance. I wouldn't dare call anyone on the spur of the moment."

I have a nine-year-old friend named Nick who signed up to play baseball. He went to every practice and worked hard with his coaches. But his first game was a disaster. He struck out every time he got up to bat. He became so flustered that he botched every play in the field too.

Completely humiliated, Nick locked himself in his bedroom that night. He refused to talk to anyone. School the next day was terrible. There weren't really that many kids who had seen the game, but Nick was certain that everyone was laughing at him behind his back. He wanted nothing more than to get home and lock himself in his room.

But to his surprise, his older brother Aaron was waiting for him after school. Aaron drove him to the park and, for the next hour, helped Nick with his hitting. He helped him with his stance, soft-tossed balls for him to swing at, and then put Nick behind the plate and pitched to him.

The next day they worked out again. And the next. And the next time Nick played, he got a hit his first time up to bat. Then he got another. And another.

Suddenly filled with confidence, Nick began chasing balls down in the field too. He was having fun, and the more fun he had, the better he played. Not only that, but his enthusiasm spread to his teammates too, firing everyone up like a bunch of firecrackers.

All because he had an older brother who cared enough to help him through a tough time.

"You really don't know *anyone* you could ask?"

"Are you kidding? I'm the world's shyest kid! Even if I *did* know someone, I wouldn't dare ask them out at the last minute like this."

Emily thought for a moment. "Well, my friend Kayla has a little sister. Would you like me to see if she's doing anything?"

"Is she cute?"

"*Ammon!*"

"I mean, do you really think she might go out with me?"

Emily made a few phone calls and ended up finding a date for her little brother. And the two not only had a wonderful time, but they ended up becoming great friends too.

"Emily and I have always been close," Ammon told me. "And I've always thought she was pretty great. But that was the first time I realized how really awesome having an older sister can be."

There are few things that impress me as much as young people who get along with their brothers and sisters. And I can't think of anything that would be more wonderful than having a family where brothers and sisters are one another's best friends.

When Nephi went to obtain the brass plates from Laban, Laman and Lemuel went with him. I know that Nephi could have gotten the plates easier, faster, and with a lot fewer problems (and headaches!) if he'd just gone by himself.

But the Lord wanted the older brothers to go anyway.

Why?

Maybe because he—like Nephi—wanted to give them every chance he could. Maybe he wanted them to learn from Nephi's example. And maybe Nephi had things to learn from them too. (Like, maybe, how not to do things!)

So how does that apply to you?

How should you treat your brothers and sisters when your parents want you to spend time with them?

Should you fuss and pull faces? Or should you go out of your way to make them feel wanted and welcome?

And I know many who are. I have a young friend named Ryan, for instance, who is constantly telling me about his younger brother.

"Josh is so cool," he once told me. "And you oughtta see him play basketball! He's only ten, but he's already a better ball player than I ever was."

What Ryan didn't mention was that Josh excelled at sports partly because Ryan spent so much time practicing with him. And partly because Josh idolized Ryan and worked hard to be just like him.

Now, I'm sure that *your* brothers and sisters are all perfect and wonderful, right? (If they're like *you*, your parents probably have to turn off their halos at night so everyone can sleep!)

But even if things aren't always so rosy, consider what things were like for Nephi.

We first meet Nephi's older brothers Laman and Lemuel in the fifth verse of 1 Nephi chapter two. By verse eleven they're already murmuring, complaining, whining, and making life miserable for everyone.

You already know that the Deadly Duo didn't qualify for any Brothers of the Year awards. But look at how rotten they really were:

EXHIBIT ONE: "Wherefore Laman and Lemuel did speak many hard words unto us, their younger brothers, and they did smite us even with a rod" (1 Nephi 3:28).

EXIBHIT TWO: "And it came to pass that when I, Nephi, had spoken these words unto my brethren, they were angry with me. And it came to pass that they did lay their hands upon me . . . and they did bind me with cords, for they sought to take away my life, that they might leave me in the wilderness to be devoured

No matter what shenanigans Laman and Lemuel pulled, Nephi was always quick to forgive them.

Why?

I think it's because Nephi believed in their potential. He didn't focus on how bad they were . . . he kept thinking about how good they could become.

Was that silly?

Well, consider Alma the Younger and the four sons of Mosiah. They were every bit as rotten as Laman and Lemuel. But they repented and became awesome, inspiring, powerful missionaries.

I think Nephi knew—and hoped—that Laman and Lemuel could one day repent and turn their lives around like that. And I believe that's one reason he never gave up on them.

by wild beasts" (1 Nephi 7:16). (They were going to leave him to be *devoured*? By wild *beasts*? Is it just me, or does that sound like, really, really mean?)

EXHIBIT THREE: "And it came to pass that they were angry with me *again*, and sought to lay hands upon me" (1 Nephi 7:19, emphasis added).

EXHIBIT FOUR: "And Laman said unto Lemuel and also unto the sons of Ishmael: Behold, let us slay our father, and also our brother Nephi" (1 Nephi 16:37).

EXHIBIT FIVE: "They were angry with me, and were desirous to throw me into the depths of the sea" (1 Nephi 17:48).

EXHIBIT SIX: "Behold, they were angry with me . . . And it came to pass that Laman and Lemuel did take me and bind me with cords, and they did treat me with much harshness" (1 Nephi 18:10–11).

EXHIBIT SEVEN: "Behold, their anger did increase against me, insomuch that they did seek to take away my life" (2 Nephi 5:2).

Boy!

Being Nephi wasn't all that easy!

And you have to be impressed with Nephi's reaction. Despite everything his brothers did to him—my word, they tried to murder him *four* different times!—he was always quick to forgive them. Not only that, but he also continued to teach them—and "exhort" them—*trying* to get them to do better.

In the end, it took a direct warning from the Lord before Nephi realized he was fighting a lost cause. And it wasn't until then that he finally took his family and left (see 2 Nephi 5:5).

Now, is there a moral to *that* story?

There will be times when you have conflicts with your brothers and sisters. You might have arguments, disagreements, or moments of tension. When you do, ask yourself this:

Would the Lord rather have you win the argument?

Or would he want you to keep the peace?

When those tough times come up, be courageous. Don't insist on proving that you're right or on getting your own way. Do what you can to be the peacekeeper. Look for ways to ease the tension. Do what you can to make peace and to keep everyone happy.

If you have brothers or sisters, you probably feel moments of tension with them. It's normal to have disagreements and misunderstandings from time to time. But no matter how difficult things seem, they'll never be as difficult as what Nephi endured.

You know, no matter what Lehi's family was experiencing, Nephi *always* tried to make things better. When the family left their home to live in the wilderness, Nephi had a good attitude.

When Lehi asked Nephi and his brothers to return to Jerusalem—a round trip of about 360 miles—Nephi immediately said yes.

Whenever the family became tired or discouraged during their time in the wilderness, Nephi offered encouragement.

When his brothers lacked faith, Nephi tried to motivate and encourage them.

When his brothers had trouble understanding the words of the Lord, Nephi taught them.

When times were tough, Nephi always set a good example.

There are a lot of powerful lessons in Nephi's books. But notice that again and again, Nephi's story revolves around his relationships with his family.

You think there's a *message* there?

As Moroni chose the stories he included in his work, do you think he ever thought, *Those young people in the latter day need to know how important it is to love their family. They need to read this!*

When I became a pilot, I learned that there are four forces that act on an airplane as it flies. *Weight* and *drag* pull the plane down, holding it back. *Lift* and *thrust* push the plane up and *forward*.

Now, in your family—with your brothers and sisters—are you the weight and the drag, holding them back, keeping them from being their best?

Or are you the lift and thrust, helping them along, boosting them upward, pushing them forward and helping them to be the best they can?

Are you happy with your answer?

Is your Heavenly Father?

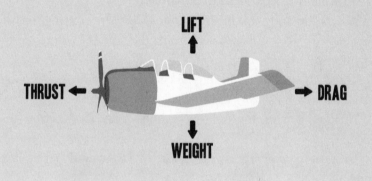

Now, your family is going to hit occasional bumps in the road too. Things might come up that cause a little friction. When they do, be like Nephi! Be the one with a good attitude! Be the one with a smile. Be the one who supports your parents. Be the one who encourages everyone else!

And think about this: suppose you were a champion weight lifter and that you were able to lift a hundred-pound barbell over your head.

It would be pretty cool, huh?

And suppose you had a friend who could also lift a hundred pounds over *his* head. Together, you should be able to lift . . . what?

Two hundred pounds?

No!

In fact, according to the laws of physics, when two weight lifters work together, they can actually lift three or four *times* the amount

Be assured that as you try to help your family, your Heavenly Father will notice. Even if your brothers or sisters don't respond, your Father in Heaven will still see your efforts. He will appreciate you for trying, and he will bless you for it!

four *times* the amount either one could lift by himself. So two people, each able to lift one hundred pounds, could together lift three hundred or four hundred pounds!

So what does that have to do with you?

When you and your brothers and sisters are working together, you're able to accomplish several *times* the amount you could possibly do by yourselves.

Think about that. Just imagine being able to finish your chores three or four times *faster* than usual.

Imagine getting the yard work done *faster* (and better) than usual!

Imagine getting the garage cleaned faster, and better, than usual.

And it doesn't just apply to chores and yard work. Imagine a family vacation being three or four times more *exciting* than usual.

Imagine family home evening being more *uplifting* than usual.

Imagine a family outing being more *fun* than usual.

Imagine a family being more supportive, more successful, more fun, more exciting, more . . . well, more of whatever you want! I think that's one of the reasons the Church puts so much emphasis on families.

And if your family isn't quite to the everyone-has-a-halo stage yet, *you can be the one who gets it started*! You can be the spark (or the bulldozer) who gets everyone in line and moving in the right direction!

Not sure what to do?

Here are a few ideas:

- When everyone's tired and grumpy, tell a joke! Sing a song!

If you have little brothers or sisters, be a good example for them! Let them tag along with you and your friends once in a while. Believe it or not, they idolize you. They watch you and follow your example. So don't think of them as pests. Enjoy the attention!

Remember that these are all little things but that doing them will pile boatloads of blessings into your spiritual bank account!

And your Heavenly Father will notice and appreciate your efforts.

Tickle someone! Break out the ice cream! Do *something* to break the ice, relieve the stress, and cheer everyone up again.

- When your parents plan family outings or activities, be supportive. Act excited, even if it's not really your idea of fun. (Remember that a trip to the bowling alley is not really a chance to improve your footwork or practice nailing the 7-10 split. It's an opportunity to spend time together as a family!) Keep in mind

If you have older brothers or sisters, be submissive when your parents leave them in charge. (Treat them the way you'd like younger brothers and sisters to treat you when you're left in charge!) Listen to them and be respectful. Make their jobs easier by being supportive (and by not causing problems).

that it's not *what* you're doing that's important; it's the fact that you're doing something together, becoming closer as a family.
- If one of your sisters is grumpy or having a bad day, be understanding! Look for ways to help or to cheer her up.
- When you have a problem or conflict with your brothers or sisters, shake it off. Let them have their way! Quietly do the dishes, mow the lawn, or take out the garbage. Whatever the issue is, try to resolve it . . . even if it means not getting your own way! Like Nephi, try to be the peacemaker in the family.

- Be supportive when times are tough. If one of your brothers is going through a hard time, try to be the bright spot in his life. Let him know you care. Show him that he can count on you for support and encouragement.

  Better yet, try doing something in secret to boost his spirits. Do one of his least favorite chores for him. Leave a note on his pillow or a candy bar in his gym shoe. Look for fun, unusual ways to brighten his day and help him out.

Take a look at the chart below. It's a good way to make the most of your relationships with your brothers and sisters.

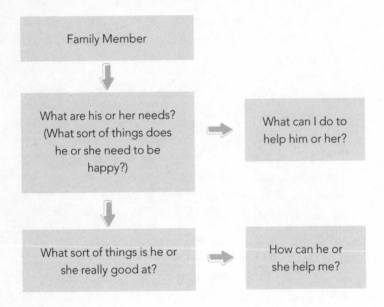

Quick note, here. A young woman once asked me about the last box, "How can he or she help me?"

"Isn't that kind of selfish?" she asked.

Not at all!

After all, isn't that one of the purposes of families? To help one another?

And doesn't it make *you* feel good when *you* help someone else?

Sure it does! And by allowing someone to do something for you, you're giving them an opportunity to feel better about themselves.

So don't think of it as something selfish. Think of it as an opportunity to become closer together and to give your brother or sister a chance to do something nice.

Anyway, here's the way my friend Sariah used the chart with her brother Tyler:

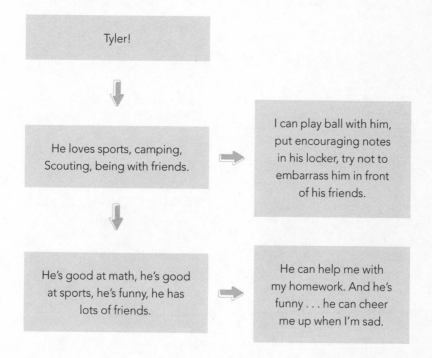

There . . . see how it works? Okay. Now, choose one of your brothers or sisters (Or—if you're an only child—you can choose a parent, a cousin, or maybe a friend or neighbor. You get extra points if it's someone you might be having difficulties with.) and fill in the following chart:

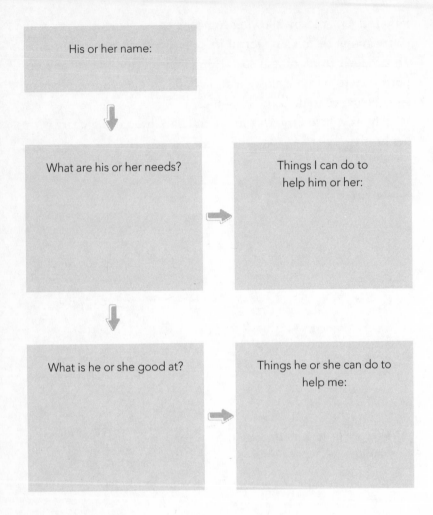

There you go!

Now the most important thing is this: *you have to take action*! Today! None of this does any good if you don't try it. So take a second and take a good look at your chart. Then think of one thing you can do today—*today*!—to bless or help the person you have listed.

Remember that it's no accident that you have the brothers and sisters you do. Your Father in Heaven didn't just choose names out of a hat when he created your family. I believe that you're here—together—for a reason. You're here to help them, and they're here to help you.

And believe me, when you're doing your best to make your family work—when you're doing your best to be good to your brothers and sisters—your Heavenly Father will notice. He'll bless your efforts. And he'll reward you for trying.

And if your brothers and sisters don't respond?

That's okay!

Don't give up!

As hard as Nephi tried to encourage them, Laman and Lemuel didn't always respond either. But that didn't keep Nephi from trying. It didn't keep him from being the best example he could. It didn't keep him from being the best brother he could.

You can be like Nephi!

You can be a fantastic brother or sister.

You can be the link that holds your family together.

Remember that your Father in Heaven is keeping score. He'll see the efforts you make. And he'll bless you for them.

I was once visiting with a young woman named Savannah and asked who her best friend was.

"Melissa," she said without hesitation.

"Melissa . . ." I had to think for a moment before I caught on. "Your sister Melissa?"

She nodded.

That is so cool! I thought. *Being best friends with your own brothers and sisters.*

You may or may not have a relationship like that. Some brothers and sisters make it harder than others. (Remember Laman and Lemuel?) But the important thing is this: Are you doing your part? Are you doing the best you can to make things work? If not, what's one thing you could do today to be a better brother or sister? (Now go do it!)

BEING A GREAT BROTHER OR SISTER CHECKUP

Suppose your brothers and sisters got together and gave you a report card. How would they grade *you* on each of the following?

Being a good example	A	B	C	D	E
Spending time with them	A	B	C	D	E
Helping them with problems	A	B	C	D	E
Doing your share of the chores	A	B	C	D	E
Being their friend	A	B	C	D	E
Sharing with them	A	B	C	D	E
Helping them feel important	A	B	C	D	E
Helping them feel loved	A	B	C	D	E
Being supportive when times are tough	A	B	C	D	E

Now . . . can you think of one thing you could do today to improve your score?

Please go do it! And do it now!

DO YOU HAVE A BROTHER OR SISTER WHO'S STRUGGLING

with his or her homework? Or having trouble with friends? Or worried about something? What's something you could do to help him or her?

_____

_____

_____

_____

Go do it today!

NEPHI'S OLDER BROTHERS WEREN'T ALWAYS EASY TO GET

along with. But Nephi never gave up on them. Consider his example:

- He prayed for his brothers (1 Nephi 2:18).

- He taught his brother Sam, helping to build and strengthen his testimony (1 Nephi 2:17).

- He tried to teach his older brothers Laman and Lemuel, even when they wouldn't listen to him (1 Nephi 2:18).

- He encouraged his brothers when times were tough (1 Nephi 3:15–16, 21).

- He encouraged them to be faithful and obedient (1 Nephi 4:1–2).

- He set a good example for them (1 Nephi 7:8).

- He forgave them again and again and again . . . even though they were really rotten to him at times (How many times did they beat him? Tie him up? Try to kill him?) (1 Nephi 7:21).

- He chewed them out when they needed a good tongue-lashing (1 Nephi 7:8–15).

THREE

AVALANCHE DOG ... TO THE RESCUE!
WHEN DOORS CLOSE IN YOUR LIFE

The search-and-rescue dog sat perched on the snowmobile like a hood ornament as the machine raced across the ridgetop. Clouds of fresh powder flew up from the skis, covering Trace and her driver as they zoomed along.

Minutes earlier, a cornice of snow had broken from the ridge, triggering an avalanche. A snowboarder had been caught in the sliding snow . . . and maybe more than one. Trace and her handler had been training nearby when the snow slid and now—with lives on the line—were racing to help.

They quickly reached the top of the saddle and came to a stop. Trace jumped from the seat and sat obediently, quivering with excitement, waiting for the command to search.

Trace had been trained to treat rescue work as a game like hide and seek. Whenever she found a volunteer or piece of clothing hidden in the snow, she received treats and praise.

And she was good at it.

But today she seemed to know that it was more than a game. She quivered expectantly as her handler studied the scene. Becoming impatient, Trace barked.

The patrolman took another second to be sure the scene was safe, then pointed down the hill.

"Trace! Search!"

Trace instantly bounded down the slope. Her sensitive nose

sifted through the thousands of scents lingering over the snow. She quickly found the one she wanted and homed in on it like a guided missile. Within minutes she'd found the right spot. She barked, then buried her nose in the snow, pawing furiously.

Her handler skied to the spot with a long pole that he pushed deep into the snow. He felt resistance, found another spot, and tried again.

"Down here!" he shouted. "I've got him!"

By now more rescuers had arrived. They shot down the slope and began digging feverishly.

Trace, meanwhile, began searching again, looking for anyone else who might have been caught in the slide. Shouts up the hill indicated that rescuers had found the first victim . . . who was still alive!

Ski patrolmen, sheriff's deputies, and other rescuers eventually formed a line and probed the entire snowfield, searching for anyone Trace might have missed. But the dog was good. She hadn't missed anyone. She'd found the missing snowboarder, and she'd found him in time to save his life.

Trace was the undisputed hero of the day. Her quick action, focus, and obedience had saved a life. And later she even received a medal for her service.

The medal didn't mean anything to her, of course. She *loved* to work! She loved being out on the snow, and she loved the praise and attention she received for doing her job.

From the moment Trace began training to become a rescue dog, her handlers realized she was special. She was obedient. She was energetic. She was eager to please. She loved to work. She had a good temperament. She was able to focus on her job, ignoring distractions, sniffing out targets faster than any other dog on the mountain. It was almost as if she'd been born to be a rescue dog.

She had a *great* future in search and rescue.

But less than a month after finding the buried snowboarder, she was hit by a reckless skier. A sharp ski cut the tendons of her back leg. The vet was able to repair much of the damage, but the injury was too severe to ever heal completely: it meant Trace would limp for the rest of her life.

And just like that, her career in search and rescue was over.

The next winter, as other dogs began working on the snow, Trace was left behind at the medical clinic at the bottom of the

One day a ten-year-old boy named Braden came to the hospital. He'd been in and out of hospitals his whole life, and he was angry. He was angry at his illness. Angry at life. Angry at his parents. Angry at everyone who tried to help him.

One day, as he was sulking in the rec room, Trace walked in with a chew toy.

"Go away!" Braden grumped.

Trace dropped the toy at Braden's feet.

"I said, 'Go away!'"

Trace just waited patiently.

"I said, 'Go away!'"

Braden picked up the toy and threw it as far as he could.

Trace bounded after it, bringing it back and dropping it at Braden's feet. She woofed softly as if asking, "C'mon . . . is that all you've got?"

Braden fake-threw the toy. Trace bounded away, looked around for a moment, then trotted back. Her tail wagged gently as if she were saying, "Okay, you got me good that time!"

Within a few minutes, the two were playing happily, and it wasn't long before other kids joined in, playing a boisterous game of keep-away.

From that day on, Braden changed. His attitude changed. He made friends. His health began to improve. He was getting better in both body and spirit. When he finally left the hospital, he had hugs for all his new friends and for all the doctors and nurses at the hospital.

But the biggest hug of all—and the most tears—were for Trace . . . the therapy dog who'd made the difference.

Trace was able to bless hundreds of children, something she never could have done if the door to rescue work hadn't closed in her life.

mountain. Even though she was allowed inside the clinic, she spent most of her time outside, where she'd look up at the snowy mountain as if longing to be back in action.

It was all really sad. But—long story short—a prominent doctor adopted Trace, taking her to a children's hospital. There she became a "therapy dog," playing with sick children in the hospital recreation area.

And just like that, Trace had a new career. Rather than saving one or two people in a lifetime, she was suddenly helping dozens of sick and injured children every single day.

When Trace was injured, a huge door closed in her life. But eventually another door opened.

Yes, something bad happened to her.

But something even better resulted.

Sarah had been a cheerleader since the fourth grade. But when her high school was invited to compete nationally, she learned that she'd have to begin performing on Sundays.

Not only that, but her team began practicing on Monday nights too, which interfered with family home evening. When Sarah told her coach that she couldn't participate on Sundays or Monday nights, she was cut from the team.

"The coach told me that she didn't have any choice," Sarah said. "There were a lot of girls on the team—all with different religious backgrounds—and it was impossible to accommodate everyone's schedules."

Sarah was devastated! She loved cheering! For years and years, her whole life had revolved around cheering!

But after she was cut from the team, she tried out for the school musical . . . and landed a leading role. And just that fast, she knew she'd found a new "home."

"I had no idea drama could be so fun!" she said. "I loved cheering, but I found that I loved drama even more!

"Besides"—Her eyes twinkled as she said this—"in drama there are a lot more boys!"

Nephi doesn't tell us much about his life in Jerusalem. But because his family was wealthy (Nephi said they owned gold, silver, and all manner of riches and other precious things), he probably had a pretty good life. He probably lived in a nice home. He probably had nice clothes. I think he had good friends . . . and he probably had a lot of them.

What I'm getting at is that Nephi's life was pretty good. He had a nice home, plenty of precious things, good friends. And when Lehi took his family into the wilderness, Nephi had to leave all that behind. The door closed on that part of his life. And the door didn't just close, it slammed shut so hard that it shook the house. (And I wouldn't be surprised if a huge DON'T COME BACK! sign sprang up in the front yard.)

But Nephi didn't waste time thinking about any of that. He didn't waste time thinking about all the cool things he was missing. He didn't waste time thinking about all the fun things he was leaving behind.

Why?

Because Nephi knew something important. He knew that the Lord never closes a door without opening another one.

Imagine sitting in the driver's seat of your family's car. See the windshield? It's a lot bigger than the rearview mirror, isn't it? That's because cars are designed to be driven forward, not backward.

As they traveled through the wilderness, Nephi didn't dwell on the great life he'd left behind in Jerusalem. Instead, he focused on all the fantastic adventures he had ahead of him.

When doors close in your life, don't waste time dwelling on those things you're missing out on. Instead, keep your head up. Put a smile on your face. Keep your eyes forward. Focus on all the fantastic things waiting ahead of you.

Think about the friends you haven't met yet.

Think about the opportunities waiting just around the next corner.

Think about all the potential, the surprises, and the adventures your Heavenly Father has in store for you!

Yes, he had to leave a lot behind. And yes, he had to forsake a good home to live in the wilderness.

He had to give up good food to hunt his own (which he had to eat raw, by the way).

He had to leave behind all his friends, having no one to hang out with but Sam and a couple of goofy older brothers.

But the Lord had something else in mind for Nephi. The Lord closed the door on something good, but he opened a door to something better.

He led Nephi to the promised land.

He gave Nephi lessons and experiences that—as we read about them in the Book of Mormon—are still blessing people thousands of years later.

Nephi had been a prosperous, popular, energetic teenager. But he ended up as a king.

A *king*!

And for centuries, his righteous descendants were called by *his* name . . . "Nephites."

Yes, the Lord closed a door in Nephi's life. But he opened a door that was more fabulous and more fantastic than Nephi could have ever imagined.

Now, there will be times when doors close in your life too. And it often hurts when they do. You might lose a friend. Your family might move, leaving behind friends, schools, clubs, or teams. You might lose a job or a place in a school club or athletic team.

But I believe that the Lord never closes a door without opening another one. And if that door closes he'll open *another* one. If all the doors close, he'll start opening the windows!

When I was in high school, I spent a summer working at Boy Scout camp. After I returned from my mission to Japan, I went back for another summer. And then I went back again and again and again, summer after summer after summer. Over the years, I

> When doors close in your life, your Heavenly Father will open others. If all the doors close, he'll start opening the windows!

worked at Boy Scout camps, Cub Scout camps, survival camps, rock-climbing camps, cross-country-ski camps, outdoor leadership camps, aquatics bases, and high adventure bases.

And I can't tell you how much fun I had!

My experiences at Scout camp were some of the best of my life! I made more friends than I can count and had more fun than I ever thought possible.

Finally, though, after more than twenty years of summer camping, it all came crashing to a close. And I . . . felt . . . *awful*!

As spring came, and then summer, I felt like my whole world had fallen apart. There was suddenly an enormous hole in my life. And I had no idea how to fill it.

A huge door had closed in my life, and I was miserable.

Since I didn't have much to do that first summer, I signed up for an Emergency Medical Technician (EMT) class. I have no idea why I did that. It was just something to do. But I had fun. I made friends with many of the other students and looked forward to going to class every day.

That winter—after I earned my EMT badge—I joined the National Ski Patrol. And just like that, I knew I'd found a new home. I can't tell you how much *fun* I had. My second year I was voted "Hardest Working Patroller." Two different times I was named "Patrolman of the Month." My fifth year I was named "Outstanding Patroller." My sixth year I was named "Outstanding Patroller" again. And my seventh year, I became the assistant patrol director at my resort.

I don't say those things to brag but to show how much fun—and how much success—I was having. And the thing I told people again and again was that I wished I'd started patrolling twenty years earlier.

> Stay positive when doors close in your life. Keep a smile on your face. And then be on the lookout for another door to open.
>
> Rather than being unhappy when things don't turn out the way you want, focus on all the great things your Heavenly Father has planned ahead of you!

The point is, I *never* would have become an EMT and joined the ski patrol if the Lord hadn't closed the door on Scout camping.

Yeah, I was sad when the door closed on summer camp. But I truly believe that door closed in my life so I could join the ski patrol.

The next time a door closes in your life, don't spend time thinking about what you're missing. Instead, be on the lookout for another door to open. Keep your eyes peeled! Be ready! Get excited, 'cause it's gonna happen!

Know that your Heavenly Father has great plans for you. And as you remain faithful and patient, you'll find doors leading to greater and greater things.

I truly believe that when the Lord closes doors in your life, it's because he has even greater things planned for you!

Remember Joseph? (The one with the rock-'em, sock-'em, razzle-dazzle, check-me-out, and glow-in-the-dark dreamcoat?) Think about all the doors that slammed shut in his life . . . and all of the fantastic things that happened because of them:

President Howard W. Hunter once said, "Doors close regularly in our lives, and some of those closings cause genuine pain and heartache. But I do believe that where one such door closes, another opens (and perhaps more than one), with hope and blessings in other areas of our lives that we might not have discovered otherwise" ("The Opening and Closing of Doors," *Ensign*, Nov. 1987, 54).

THE LIFE AND TIMES OF JOSEPH IN EGYPT!

Jacob has twelve sons, but the youngest—Joseph—is his all-time favorite. And for Joseph, life . . . was . . . *goooood*!

Joseph's brothers become so jealous that they sell him as a slave, telling his father that he was killed and eaten by an "evil beast."

WHAMMO!

A *huge* door closes in Joseph's life!

Joseph is taken to Egypt, but he decides to make the best of the situation. Things work out so good that his master promotes him. Next thing you know, Joseph's running the house. Wow! Joseph goes from living in the desert to being chief-of-staff to Potipher, the captain of Pharaoh's guards. And once again, life . . . is . . . *gooooood*!

Hard times are coming to Egypt, and Pharaoh needs someone he can count on to help. Someone who can withstand adversity. Someone who won't fold or buckle under pressure. Who does he choose? Joseph! And Joseph becomes ruler over all of Egypt, second only to Pharaoh himself.

Joseph's life falls to pieces, forcing him to start all over . . . *again*! But he decides to make the best of things. He works hard and becomes the best prisoner in the whole prison! He's actually put in charge of all the other prisoners!

Joseph is accused of a crime he didn't commit and is thrown into prison. *Kaaablooey*! Another door slams shut in Joseph's life!

Wow!

What an *amazing* story!

And the key is this: if his naughty brothers hadn't closed that first door in his life, Joseph *never* would have gone to Egypt.

If Joseph hadn't gone to Egypt, he *never* would have served Potipher.

If Joseph hadn't served Potipher, he *never* would have been thrown in prison.

Not all of Joseph's experiences were fun at the time. Can you imagine what it was like being sold as a slave? And to complete strangers?

Can you imagine being thrown in prison? Especially when you haven't done anything wrong?

But Joseph knew those things were happening for a reason. He knew that the Lord was preparing him for even greater things to come. When his brothers later apologized for being so rotten, Joseph said something interesting. He said, "Hey, don't worry about it, guys. The Lord planned all this for me . . . and he did it for a reason!" (See Genesis 45:5, 7–8).

If he hadn't been thrown in prison, he *never* would have met Pharaoh. He *never* would have risen to such an awesome, incredible position!

Yes, doors closed in Joseph's life. But every single time something went wrong, something even *better* came along!

And all those little roadblocks along the way turned into stepping stones, teaching Joseph lessons that led him to even greater, more fantastic things!

When you look at it that way, being sold into Egypt was actually one of the best things that ever happened to him. Being thrown into prison even turned out to be a blessing in disguise. As the Lord said to Joseph Smith, all those bad things gave him experience, and they worked out for his good! (See D&C 122:7.)

THE LORD CAN OPEN DOORS THAT NO ONE CAN EVER SHUT!

When I was in college, I was once flying a small airplane from Ogden, Utah, to Provo. It had been a long day, and I was tired, cramped, and sore.

As I was passing Salt Lake City, air traffic control suddenly called.

"Cessna Seven Two Kilo, turn left to heading niner-zero degrees and maintain altitude."

"New heading of niner zero degrees," I said, turning the plane and lining up my compass. "Roger."

Great, I thought, looking around. *I wonder what's going on.*

The trouble was, I wasn't flying toward home anymore, and the longer I was on this new heading, the longer it would be before I got home.

On top of that, I was now flying straight toward a tall, jagged mountain . . . and I wasn't flying high enough to go over the top. I was just beginning to worry a little bit when the air traffic controller called me back.

"Cessna Seven Two Kilo, resume original heading, maintain altitude, and have a good day."

> "Wherefore, ye must press *forward* with a steadfastness in Christ, having a perfect brightness of hope, and a love of God and of all men. Wherefore, if ye shall press *forward*, feasting upon the word of Christ, and endure to the end, behold, thus saith the Father: Ye shall have eternal life" (2 Nephi 31:20, emphasis added).

I didn't know what it was all about. But it didn't matter. The controller was sitting in front of a radar screen where he could see the whole picture. There might have been a bigger, faster plane

> If you have received your patriarchal blessing, there are sure to be promises of great blessings and fantastic opportunities still ahead of you. So when doors close in your life, remember Nephi. Rather than dwell upon those things you're missing out on, look forward to all the wonderful surprises and blessings the Lord has planned ahead for you!

behind me, for instance, and maybe he just needed me to move long enough for it to pass me.

You need to remember that your Heavenly Father sees the whole picture too. And it's not important that you know the reason for every little setback and problem that comes up in your life. You might feel bad now when doors close in your life. But years from now you might look back and actually be *glad* that they did!

You may not understand it all now, but that's okay. That's what faith is all about. You need to learn to trust your Heavenly Father, believing that he's in control and that he'll make sure that everything works out for your good.

President Howard W. Hunter once said, "At various times in our lives, probably at repeated times in our lives, we do have to acknowledge that God knows what we do not know and sees what we do not see. 'For my thoughts are nor your thoughts, neither are your ways my ways, saith the Lord' (Isaiah 55:8)" ("The Opening and Closing of Doors," *Ensign*, Nov. 1987, 54).

President Hunter also said, "I have taken great comfort over the years in this explanation of some of life's pain and disappointment. I take [great] comfort that the greatest of men and women, including the Son of God, have faced . . . opposition in order to better understand the contrast between righteousness and wickedness, holiness and misery, good and bad. From out of the dark, damp confinement of Liberty Jail, the Prophet Joseph Smith learned that if we are called to pass through tribulation, it is for our growth and experience and will ultimately be for our good (see D&C 122:5–8). Where one door shuts, another opens, even for a prophet in prison" ("The Opening and Closing of Doors," *Ensign*, Nov. 1987, 54).

When doors close in your life, don't give up. When you reach dead ends, don't quit. Instead, find a different door and push forward! Like Nephi, focus on the adventures and opportunities that are still ahead of you.

And don't look at closed doors as the end. Look at them as new beginnings. Remember that your Heavenly Father loves you.

He has better things in store for you. And the really exciting thing is, you never know when or where they'll show up.

Alma was a young priest in the court of the wicked King Noah. He wasn't living righteously at the time, but he was a rising star in the land.

But when Abinadi preached to the king, Alma was touched by the Spirit. He *knew* that Abinadi was preaching the truth. He pleaded with King Noah to spare Abinadi's life, making Noah so angry that he sent servants to slay him.

Alma had to flee for his life, and *whammo!* A huge door slammed shut in his life.

Alma—who had been King Noah's rising star—was now poor, homeless, living on the lam. But he began preaching to anyone who would listen. More and more people came to hear him and to be baptized. Alma organized the Church of Christ. A new door had opened for him, and things were suddenly looking up again.

But King Noah discovered what Alma was up to and sent his army to destroy him. Alma and his people were forced to flee into the wilderness.

Whammo!

Another door slammed shut in Alma's life.

But Alma and his people refused to give up. They began tilling the ground and building a city. Things were beginning to look good again. But then—oh, *man!*—along came the Lamanites. They began persecuting Alma's people, forcing them to flee again.

After all this, Alma *finally* found the land of Zarahemla, where King Benjamin welcomed them.

Alma had doors close on him time and time again. But his experiences—and his son's—eventually became some of the most remarkable, inspirational, powerful lessons and sermons in the Book of Mormon.

FOUR

OUCH! SETBACK! I'VE BROKEN MY BOW!
DEALING WITH SETBACKS

"Well, this is just *great*."

Elder Nielsen looked up from his bicycle tire, which was flatter than a Boy Scout's first campout pancake. He pursed his lips as if trying to remember a Harry Potter–type charm that might work on bicycle tires, then reached up to brush the rain from his hair.

"Well, Elder . . . do you have any suggestions?"

I looked up at the sky, trying to gauge the ferocity of the storm. "Not really." I scrunched my shoulders as the rain fell a little harder. "But I have a question."

"Yeah? What's that?"

"How long can you tread water?"

Elder Nielsen laughed.

Which didn't surprise me: Elder Nielsen was *always* laughing. He was the happiest, smiliest, most enthusiastic, optimistic missionary I'd ever worked with. Nothing ever bothered him. He radiated such positive energy that he could cheer people up just being in the same room with them.

I sincerely thought that if happiness was money, Elder Nielsen could have bought Texas.

I flinched as a crack of thunder boomed over the mountain rice fields, snapping me back to reality. I'd been on my mission to Japan for just less than six months, and this was the worst storm I'd ever seen.

It hadn't started out that way. When Elder Nielsen and I left our apartment to meet with one of our favorite families, the rain had been a pleasant drizzle. But as we pedaled our bikes through the rice paddies, the drizzle became more steady.

The steady rain became a torrent.

The torrent became a downpour.

The downpour became such a cold, icy deluge that I suddenly knew what it must be like standing beneath a waterfall.

And then, right when it looked like things couldn't get any worse, the rear tire of Elder Nielsen's bike blew out.

It almost seemed as if something was trying to keep us from our meeting.

I looked at my good-natured companion, who was standing with his hands on his hips, looking around as the rain ran through his hair.

"What are you looking for?" I asked.

"Noah," he said. "With all this rain, I can't help thinking the ole ark's going to come floating by any minute now . . . maybe we could hitch a ride."

When the Apostle Paul was shipwrecked, he was gathering firewood when a snake flew out of the woodpile and latched onto his hand. (Okay, that would have freaked me right out!) But Paul (and I love the way Luke says this) simply "shook off the beast into the fire" (Acts 28:5).

He shook it off.

Everyone was certain the snakebite would kill Paul. But he surprised everyone. He simply "shook it off" and went about his business.

When things come up that threaten to hurt or discourage you, don't let them poison your spirit. Don't let them sour your attitude. Don't let them slow you down or hold you back.

Shake them off!

Laugh them off!

Look them square in the eye and ask, "Is that it? Is that all you've got? There's no way I'm gonna let that hurt me!"

He grinned, then glanced at his watch. "Well, what do you think?"

"Feel like walking?"

"Guess so."

We pushed our bikes down the road as the rain poured and the lightning flashed. But if Elder Nielsen was discouraged, he didn't show it. In fact, he began working on my spirits too.

"'I will go and do the things which the Lord hath commanded . . .'" he said, beginning a scripture.

"That's 1 Nephi 3:7," I replied. It was a game we often played. One of us would quote a scripture, and the other would name the reference. The first one to be stumped had to wash the dinner dishes.

Now it was my turn. "Wherefore, ye must press forward with a steadfastness in Christ . . ."

"Oh, puhleeeze," he said, as if disappointed I hadn't given him something more difficult. "It's 2 Nephi 31:20."

By the time we reached the Yamaguchi home, we were drenched to the skin. But Elder Nielsen never once seemed discouraged or unhappy.

And the Yamaguchi family?

Brother Yamaguchi was astounded to see us. He couldn't believe we'd brave such horrendous weather to keep our appointment. And when he learned that we'd had to walk most of the way, he was even more touched.

"Brother Yamaguchi," Elder Nielsen said in his most solemn voice, "our message is so important that I sold my car. I postponed college. I left my family and friends and came all the way to Japan to teach your family the gospel of Jesus Christ. There's no way I'm gonna let a little rain stop me now."

Elder Nielsen's attitude made a difference to me that day. And it made a difference to the Yamaguchi family too. It affected Brother Yamaguchi so deeply that he began reading the Book of Mormon even more earnestly, praying, pondering, and developing a strong testimony. I believe it was the turning point that led him to baptism.

Remember David?

As he was taking food to his brothers in the war, the giant Goliath came out to challenge the army. (See 1 Samuel 17.) The Israelites had plenty of humungous warriors. They had plenty of champions. But no one was brave enough to go up against the nine-foot Goliath.

Until David came along.

While everyone else was looking at the size of the problem, David was looking at the size of the opportunities. While everyone else was thinking Goliath was too big to fight, David was thinking, "He's too big to miss!"

I learned a lot about setbacks as a missionary. And I learned a lot about *dealing* with setbacks from my energetic companion.

Which is something I could have learned just as well from Nephi.

Remember the story? After Lehi's family had been traveling in the wilderness for a while, they stopped to rest and gather food. Things hadn't been easy for them. After all, the desert was hot.

It was dusty.

It was humid.

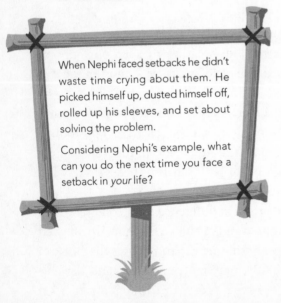

When Nephi faced setbacks he didn't waste time crying about them. He picked himself up, dusted himself off, rolled up his sleeves, and set about solving the problem.

Considering Nephi's example, what can you do the next time you face a setback in *your* life?

The scorching heat blistered the family during the day, and the desert chill froze them at night. There wasn't a lot of food. Not much water. Nothing much to do except walk . . . and walk . . . and walk (listening to Laman and Lemuel grumbling, whining, and complaining the whole time).

So the family finally stopped to take a break, rest for a bit, and find some fresh meat.

Weeeeell, that was the plan, anyway.

"And it came to pass," Nephi wrote, "that as I . . . went forth to slay food, behold, I did break my bow, which was made of fine steel; and after I did break my bow, behold, my brethren were angry with me because of the loss of my bow, for we did obtain no food.

"And it came to pass that we did return without food to our families, and being much fatigued, because of their journeying,

When Joseph was a young boy his jealous brothers sold him as a slave into Egypt (Genesis 39).

Ouch!

Huge setback!

Yes, Joseph had plenty of reasons to be discouraged, but he didn't dwell on his problems. Instead, he focused on his opportunities. He made the best of the situation, working as hard as he could and earning a position of leadership in his master's house.

But then—just as everything was working out again—he was accused of a crime he didn't commit and thrown into prison.

Ouch again!

Monster setback!

But once again, Joseph refused to dwell on his problems. He focused on his opportunities, setting about becoming the best prisoner in the prison!

Because of Joseph's unstoppable spirit, when a seven-year famine threatened to crush the country and Pharaoh needed someone he could count on—someone who wouldn't buckle under adversity—he turned to Joseph.

There will be times when you too will suffer setbacks. But—like Joseph—don't dwell on your problems. Focus instead on your opportunities. Look for the best in every situation. Look for ways to use your setback as a setup for a fantastic, rip-roaring, come-from-behind comeback!

they did suffer much for the want of food" (1 Nephi 16:18–19).

Ouch!

Huge setback!

You've got to remember that Lehi's family was wealthy. They were used to living the "good life." And now they'd spent the last umpteen weeks wandering through the desert. They were hot, tired, sore, sunburned, hungry . . .

And then—right when it looked like they might get a break and have a little fresh meat for a change—Nephi's bow snapped.

Boom!

Setback!

The whole family's hopes came crashing down like a ton of bricks.

On top of that—well, you know how it is. When times are tough, people often lose their patience and begin snapping at one another, moaning, groaning, whining, griping, grumbling, scowling, sniping, wailing, whimpering . . .

You know—just making things even more miserable for everyone.

And this time it wasn't just Laman and Lemuel. The sons of Ishmael and even Lehi himself began murmuring and complaining about everything that was going wrong.

And Nephi?

Sure, he was hungry!

Yeah, he was tired.

He was just as sunburned, sore, and disappointed as everyone else.

But it's what he did about it that made the difference.

"And it came to pass," he wrote, "that I . . . did make out of wood a bow, and out of a straight stick, an arrow; wherefore, I did arm myself with a bow and an arrow, with a sling and with stones" (1 Nephi 16:18–23).

Think about it. Nephi could have given up. He could have sat around thinking how much better off he'd be if the family had stayed in Jerusalem. He could have wallowed in self pity, feeling sorry for himself.

Remember Ammon?

As he was tending sheep with King Lamoni's servants (Alma 17), mischievous Lamanites came and scattered the flock. The king's servants were instantly afraid, believing King Lamoni would slay them all for losing his sheep. After all, that's what he'd done when things like that happened before.

Ouch!

Setback!

And Ammon . . . Just when he'd been accepted by the Lamanites and things were looking good for him, a buncha trouble makers just had to come along and ruin everything. Ammon could have given up and run away with the others. He could have become afraid and discouraged.

But that wasn't his style.

In fact, "[Ammon's] heart was *swollen with joy*; for, said he, I will show forth my power unto these my fellow servants . . . that I may win [their] hearts . . . that I may lead them to believe in my words" (Alma 17:29, emphasis added).

Wow!

What an *attitude*!

While everyone else was focusing on the size of the problem, Ammon was looking for the good in the situation. He was looking at the size of the *opportunities*!

When you face setbacks, you can do the same thing. Look for ways to turn a bad situation into something good. Look for opportunities the Lord might be placing in front of you. Sure, something bad might have happened, but something *better* might result!

But he didn't. Instead, *he went out and he did something about it! Wow. You have to admire his attitude.*

And that, I think, is one of the great lessons we can learn from Nephi. It's an example that—if you follow it—will bless and enrich your life.

As you go through life, you're bound to have challenges from time to time. Right when everything is going good, problems are likely to spring up and make things difficult.

But it's those challenges that will help you grow the most. So when the tough times come, remember Nephi. Remember his attitude as he handled his problems. "Liken" his attitude to yourself.

There's something else about Nephi's story that's always impressed me. Do you remember, for instance, what he did after making himself a new bow? He went to his father and asked, "Whither shall I go to obtain food?" (1 Nephi 16:23).

Now you've got to remember that Nephi was the outdoorsman of the family. He was the expert with the bow. He was the hunter of the family. He supplied everyone with fresh meat.

Even so, he went to his father for advice. You see, Nephi knew that Lehi was feeling discouraged. He knew it wasn't easy being the head of the family . . . especially when everyone was tired and hungry and sniping at one another (all of that made even worse by Lehi's oldest sons complaining and stirring everyone up).

So Nephi went to his father for advice. What he was really saying was, "Hey, Dad, you're doing okay. You're doing the right thing. I love you. I trust you. I have faith in you."

You see, even in the face of a monster setback, Nephi was thinking of others. He was thinking of ways to help and to lift their spirits.

What a fantastic attitude!

And you know what? You can do the same thing! The next time you hit a bump in the road, you can be the one who keeps everyone else on track. You can be the one who boosts their spirits and charges their batteries. You can be the one to "succor the

> The apostle Paul wrote to the Corinthians that our Heavenly Father will "comfort us in all our tribulation, *that we may be able to comfort them which are in any trouble*" (2 Corinthians 1:4, emphasis added).
>
> Paul was saying that when times are tough, the Lord will help us so that we can help others!
>
> I believe that if we'll do our best to help others when times our tough, our Heavenly Father will do the same for us.

weak, lift up the hands which hang down, and strengthen the feeble knees" (D&C 81:5).

Having a positive mental attitude doesn't mean you'll never have weeds in your garden. A positive mental attitude means seeing the weeds, yanking them out, and then getting on with your life. A positive mental attitude means keeping the weeds from ruining your day!

Not only *can* you do it, you *need* to do it.

So the next time a challenge or setback tries to make a mess of your life, be like Nephi.

Put a smile on your face.

Look for ways to solve the problem.

Look for ways to turn things around.

Look for new doors and opportunities.

Look for lessons to learn.

Look for ways to encourage, strengthen, and uplift those around you.

I believe that if you'll try to make the best of bad situations and if you help others through tough times, your Heavenly Father will do the same for you.

SETBACKS CHECKUP

Take a minute to read each of the questions below and then circle the number that best applies to you.

	NEVER!				ALWAYS!
When problems come up in my life, I jump right in and take care of them.	1	2	3	4	5
When I'm faced with a problem, I spend more time looking for solutions than in feeling sorry for myself.	1	2	3	4	5
When things go wrong, I focus on finding answers rather than whining.	1	2	3	4	5
Whenever things go wrong, I try looking for the bright side.	1	2	3	4	5
When problems come up, I help to lift others' spirits (rather than whining and bringing them down).	1	2	3	4	5

Whew! Now, take a deep breath and have a look at how you answered. Do you notice any patterns? If you circled lots of 4s and 5s . . . good for you! (And if you circled any 1s or 2s, this chapter is for you!)

Have you ever read a really great book or watched an exciting movie? Chances are the hero faced some pretty tough setbacks. But I bet you didn't worry too much, did you?

Why?

Because no matter how bad things seemed, no matter how bad things got, you knew that everything was going to work out in the end. (And half the fun is seeing how the good guys get themselves out of those sticky jams, isn't it?)

When you come to a road-block in your life, take a detour! If you can't move forward, turn left or turn right, but *keep moving*!

So, yeah, you're gonna go through tough times once in a while. But if you're patient, trusting your Heavenly Father, the day will come when you'll see that every problem, every setback, and every disappointment you ever had was actually part of God's great plan for you.

And believe it or not, some of your greatest challenges will eventually lead to some of your greatest blessings.

LEARN TO USE SETBACKS AS SETUPS FOR FANTASTIC COMEBACKS!

When setbacks threaten to slow you down, it's important to keep a good attitude. Keep your head up. Look for solutions. Use the following chart to keep yourself moving in the right direction:

Describe a problem or set-back that you're facing or worrying about:

_____
_____
_____
_____
_____

What's one thing you need to do to solve the problem:

_____
_____
_____
_____
_____

What's one thing you can do today to take care of that?

_____
_____
_____
_____

What's something else you can do to solve the problem?

_____
_____
_____
_____

What's something you can do today to take care of that?

_____
_____
_____
_____

Yes, this life is full of roadblocks, bumps, snags, dead ends, and challenges. And you will face setbacks once in a while. Everyone does, but that's not the point. It's what you do and how you act when times are tough that's important.

So the next time problems creep up in your life, remember Nephi: look for ways to solve the problem.

Remember David: don't focus on the size of the problem; look at the size of the opportunities.

Remember Ammon: look for ways to turn something bad into something good.

Remember Joseph: do your best to make the best of bad situations.

Remember Paul: shake off the little things.

Remember Nephi (again): look for ways to help others who might also be struggling.

Okay, this is going to sound pretty silly, but have you ever read Harry Potter? Would that have been any fun to read if Harry didn't have to deal with You-Know-Who?

Or with Snape?

Or Malfoy?

Or even Dudley?

All of those nasty characters and the problems they caused turned Harry into the champion he was! (Without them, he would have been Neville!)

Nephi had to deal with a lot of unpleasant characters and challenges too. But it's those very things that molded Nephi into the incredible man he was.

David would have remained a simple shepherd boy if it hadn't been for Goliath.

It's the very trials and challenges you face that will mold and shape and hone you into the fantastic young man or woman your Father in Heaven wants you to be.

Remember that your Heavenly Father doesn't allow bad things to happen *to* you . . . he lets them happen *for* you. So use them! Use your setbacks as setups for outrageous, monster, foot-stomping comebacks!

FIVE
TIED UP IN THE SHIP
DEALING WITH ADVERSITY

This is what it feels like to die . . .

A sickening knot filled my stomach as my truck slipped sideways over the edge of the hill. It was tipped so sharply I could see through the passenger window all the way to the bottom of the canyon.

No, no, no, I thought, praying desperately that I'd stop sliding. *No, no, noooooo . . .*

Another inch, I thought, and I'd roll. And the hill was so steep that I'd roll all the way to the bottom. I'd be squashed flat as a pancake.

Please, I pleaded. Please stop! *Please, please, pleeeeeeease . . .*

And then—at what seemed the last possible moment—the truck stopped. Hardly daring to move, I looked out the window. I was tipped at an impossible angle. My truck almost seemed to be defying gravity, hanging onto the muddy hillside by its fingernails, ready to roll at the slightest nudge.

Knowing I had no time to spare, I released my seatbelt and *caaaarrrrefully* opened the door. And then—as fast as I could—I jumped out. I ran to the other side of the road before looking back, half expecting to see my truck go tumbling down the hill.

But it sat motionless, somehow stuck in place.

I sat down on a boulder and took several deep breaths.

Wow, I thought, trying to get my heart started again. *That was close!*

I took a couple more deep breaths, trying to calm myself, then looked around.

Well . . . now *what am I gonna do?*

It was Saturday night, and I had been camping with friends. Everyone else was spending the whole weekend in the mountains, but I was leaving early so I could be home for church the next day.

The problem was that it had been raining. And as I drove up a narrow road, the rain-soaked hillside suddenly gave way beneath the weight of my truck. The truck slipped and was now hanging precariously over the edge. It looked like the slightest nudge would send it rolling into oblivion.

As I sat looking at it, I couldn't help thinking, *Man, what did I ever do to deserve this? Here I am going home so I can go to church—trying to do what's right—and look what happens to me!*

I know I shouldn't have been thinking that way. And I instantly repented, knowing that things could have been worse.

After all, I didn't roll!

I hadn't been squashed flatter'n a bug.

And I certainly wasn't dead!

Yeah, things could have been worse. They could have been a *lot* worse.

Eventually one of my friends came driving by and—long story short—we got my truck back on the road without doing a lot of damage to it. But that's not the point. I'd just learned an important lesson about adversity.

You already know that we all go through hard times once in a while. Even when we're living righteously—even when we're doing the best we can to follow the Savior—we still have trials. That's just part of life, but that's not the point. It's *what we do* and *how we act* when times are tough that's important.

Remember when Nephi and his family began their voyage in their homemade ship? After a few days at sea, Laman, Lemuel, and some of the others became rude and rowdy. When Nephi asked them to cool their jets, they became angry, tying him up and dumping him in the bottom of the ship.

"They weren't really bright, were they?" my friend Ethan asked when we were in seminary together.

"Laman and Lemuel weren't always obedient," our teacher responded charitably. "Why do you ask?"

"Well, come on," Ethan said. "They tried pushing Nephi around before, but it never worked. Remember? When they tried beating him with a rod—"

"An angel stepped in to stop them," a young woman named Amanda cut in.

"Right," Ethan said, nodding vigorously. "And when they tried tying him up—"

"The Lord gave him the strength to break free."

"Exactly!" Ethan was thumbing through his scriptures now, looking for more examples. "And then, when they wanted to throw Nephi off a cliff into the sea—"

"He shocked their socks off!"

Ethan grinned as everyone laughed, then looked up at our teacher, spreading his hands. He pulled a face as if saying *helloooo.* "What does it take to make these guys get it?"

We all laughed again. But Ethan had us thinking because this time Nephi didn't break free. No angel showed up to save the day. And either the battery was dead on his electric finger or the Lord didn't want him using it this time.

> If God had simply taken away all of Nephi's hardships, Nephi never would have been ready for greater challenges later on.

"It's like the Lord *needed* Nephi to stay tied up for a while," Amanda pointed out.

Whatever the case, the Lord hadn't forgotten Nephi, and he wasn't letting the unruly brothers off the hook. Within a few hours it started to get windy. The sea became rough. The wind got stronger. The waves became bigger. The churning sea began bouncing the ship up and down and from side to side. Water began pouring into the ship, the wind and waves threatening to shake it apart.

And for four *loooong* miserable days, Nephi remained tied up in the bottom of the ship—tied up so tightly that he couldn't move—as the ship was thrown about in the storm.

That had to have been one miserable experience. Especially for Nephi, who was as faithful as the day was long and who didn't deserve to be treated so bad. There are a lot of things he could have been thinking as the ship bounced around in the storm, and Ethan once listed a few of them:

- "Hey, I thought the Lord was supposed to be looking out for me! What's going on here?"
- "Man, I built this ship! It's mine! I can't believe the Lord's letting them treat me like this!"
- "Like, I'm trying to do what's right for crying out loud! I'm doing my part! Why's the Lord letting them do this to me?"
- "This is soooooo unfair! What have I ever done to deserve this?"
- "Why, why, whyyyyyyy did we ever have to leave Jerusalem?"
- "You know, the next time I'm just gonna let Laban catch every one of them! And their little dog too!"

Yes, there are a lot of things Nephi could have been thinking. But he gave us an idea of what he was probably thinking in the very first verse of the Book of Mormon. Remember what he said?

> You'll never have great testimony without going through a few tests.

"Having seen many afflictions in the course of my days, nevertheless having been highly favored of the Lord in *all my days*" (1 Nephi 1:1, emphasis added).

Did you catch that? Nephi mentioned having "many afflictions" and being "favored of the Lord" in the *same sentence*. I think he was telling us that being favored of the Lord—being blessed by his Heavenly Father—didn't mean he didn't have to go through a few trials along the way.

And notice that he didn't say he was just blessed here and

Disappointments are inevitable. Feeling miserable is optional!

there or from time to time. He said he was favored in *all his days*!

A few pages later, Nephi wrote that his family "suffered many afflictions and much difficulty . . . *even so much that [he could] not write them all*" (1 Nephi 17:6, emphasis added).

They had so many problems and afflictions that he couldn't *possibly* write them all! Yet he said he was favored in *all* his days, and that *included* those four days he was tied up in the bottom of that ship.

Wow!

What an awesome way of looking at things! Nephi knew that his Heavenly Father was watching out for him, even when times were tough. He knew that the Lord was aware of him and that his Heavenly Father would give him the strength to endure whatever trials came up in his life.

The Lord told Joseph Smith to "pray always and be believing, and *all things* shall work together for your good" (D&C 90:24, emphasis added). The Lord was saying that as we strive to do what's right, all things—even our toughest trials—will turn out to be blessings in disguise.

So as miserable as it was in the bottom of that ship, Nephi probably spent those four days thinking thoughts like these:

- "Okay, I'm not having the greatest time here, but I know the Lord is watching out for me, and I will be patient . . ."
- "All right, this isn't the greatest situation. But I know I'm going to come out bigger, better, and stronger because of it."
- "No, this isn't much fun, but I trust my Heavenly Father. I *know* he will turn this around for me."

- "I . . . *know* that whosoever shall put their trust in God shall be supported in their trials, and their troubles, and their afflictions" (Alma 36:3, emphasis added). Notice that Alma didn't say that hardships would be taken away from us. Only that we would be *supported* and *strengthened* so that we could endure them.

- "Yeah, I could sit here and feel sorry for myself, but that wouldn't please my Heavenly Father. So instead, I'm going to count my blessings. . . . I'm going to 'press forward with a perfect brightness of hope.'" (2 Nephi 31:20).

- "I'll remember the example of King David, who said, 'Wait on the Lord; be of good courage, and he shall strengthen thine heart'" (Psalm 27:14).

- "The Lord's stepped in and saved me before. He must have a good reason for letting this happen, so I will be patient and have faith that everything's going to work out for me."

- "This isn't happening *to* me, it's happening *for* me. Somehow, someday, the Lord will make sure this experience turns out to be a blessing in disguise."

- "I don't care how bad this is. I don't care how much it hurts. I know that my Heavenly Father is aware of me and that he knows what I'm going through. I trust him. And I know that everything is going to work out for my good."

- "Yes, this is miserable, but now more than ever I need to set a good example . . ."

What a great attitude!

When the sons of Mosiah went on their missions to the Lamanites, the Lord said to "be patient in long-suffering and afflictions, *that ye may show forth good examples* unto them . . . and I will make an instrument of thee in my hands unto the salvation of many souls" (Alma 17:11, emphasis added).

When times are tough, there are people who will be watching you too. And your good example might be just what they need to make it through.

Think about it. Nephi could have spent those four days being miserable and feeling sorry for himself. But he chose to be patient.

When David was a young boy, the prophet Samuel anointed him to become king of Israel. A few years later, David "rocked" the giant Goliath and became an instant celebrity. Everybody knew him. Everybody *loved* him! He was like a rock star, movie star, and Super Bowl MVP all rolled into one. And for David, life . . . was . . . *goooood*!

But Saul—the current king—became jealous and decided to get rid of his young rival. David had to flee for his life, living in the mountains and hiding in caves.

David must have been confused by the way things were turning out. He could have become discouraged, thinking that maybe God had forgotten him or that the Lord was going back on his promises. He could have thought, "Hey! I'm doing my part! I'm doing what I'm supposed to! What's going on here?"

Instead, he was patient, believing that God was in charge and that he would do his part. And the Lord did, fulfilling every promise he had made.

You need to know that your Heavenly Father is aware of *you* too. He sees your troubles and your trials, and he knows exactly what you're going through. As you remain faithful, he'll give you strength to endure your challenges. He'll turn your scars into stars and your messes into messages. He'll make sure every single trial, trouble, and hardship will work out for your good (see D&C 90:24).

It's easy to be faithful when times are good. But the real growth comes when you have to endure a hardship, when you have to forgive a wrong, or when you have to choose the right.

No one likes adversity. No one likes trials. But when they come, don't give up. Don't let them get you down. Don't let them get the best of you.

Instead, remember Nephi. Do your best to look for the bright side. Do your best to be patient. Trust your Heavenly Father to strengthen you and to make those tough times work out for your good.

My tenth-grade seminary class was once reading 2 Nephi 4 (which is sometimes called "The Psalm of Nephi"). We had just read verse 30 ("Rejoice, O my heart, and cry unto the Lord, and say: O Lord, I will praise thee forever . . .") when my friend Anika raised her hand.

"Yes, Anika?"

Anika was turning pages in her Book of Mormon. "Didn't Lehi die in this chapter?"

Our teacher nodded. "Yes, he did."

Anika shook her head. "Then why was Nephi so happy?"

"Nephi felt bad," our teacher replied. "Of *course*, he did. But instead of dwelling on that, he was counting his blessings. Instead of focusing on his loss, Nephi was remembering all the wonderful things the Lord had done for him."

And that is a great strategy when things go wrong in your life too! Rather than dwell on what might be going wrong, try focusing on everything that's going right. Think of all the ways the Lord has blessed you. Remember all the times he has answered your prayers. As you do this, focusing on the blessings your Heavenly Father has given you, many of your trials and challenges will seem less important.

He chose to be faithful. He chose to trust God, believing that his Heavenly Father would help him. And the Lord did.

After four days—when the storm became so bad the tiny ship was about to break into a million pieces—the wayward brothers finally got the message. And they finally let their younger brother go.

By that time, Nephi had been tied up for so long—and so tightly—that his wrists and ankles were red, swollen, and raw. It probably hurt just touching them.

Nephi had a lot of reasons to be angry about that. He had a lot of reasons to be resentful. He had a lot of reasons to complain and murmur.

But was he mad?

No.

Angry?

No.

Resentful?

No.

Instead, Nephi praised the Lord, refusing to complain, refusing to murmur, instead thanking his Heavenly Father for all of his many blessings (1 Nephi 18:16).

What a great example! You know, it's easy to be faithful when times are good. It's easy to have a positive attitude when life is good and everything's going your way. But the real test—the true test—is showing faith, hope, and gratitude when times are tough.

One thing you already know about this life is that bad things happen . . . and, yes, they sometimes happen to good people. Sometimes they happen to really good people.

When I was your age, my family went through a bad experience. And I remember my little sister saying, "I didn't think anything like this would ever happen to us! I thought we were special!"

Note to little sister: We were special . . . and we still are. But we're still going to have our share of bad days.

And so are you. Even when you're doing the best you can to

In the Old Testament, the Lord commanded Abraham to sacrifice his son, Isaac. Abraham didn't understand why he had to do that, but he trusted his Heavenly Father. And he set out to obey his Father in Heaven. The Lord, of course, stopped him at the last second, telling Abraham that he'd passed the test.

People have often wondered why the Lord needed to test him. After all, he knew what Abraham would do. And I love the way President Hugh B. Brown responded: "Abraham," he said, "needed to learn something about Abraham." (Truman G. Madsen, *Joseph Smith the Prophet*, illustrated edition [Salt Lake City: Deseret Book, 2010], 162)

We don't always know why the Lord asks us to endure certain challenges. And we don't always need to know why. But when times are tough there are always things we can learn about ourselves.

Remember too that Nephi faced many challenges. But each one prepared and strengthened him for even greater challenges later on. Your trials will prepare and strengthen you too for adventures and trials still to come.

> The Apostle Paul wrote to the Corinthians, we are "perplexed, but not in despair" (2 Corinthians 4:8). I think Paul was saying, "No, we don't always understand why God allows certain trials and challenges into our lives. But we don't let that worry us. We know that he is God, that he has things under control, and that he knows what he's doing. We know that even our toughest trials will work out and be for our good."

be good, even when you're doing the best you can to follow the Savior, you're still going to hit a few bumps in the road. You might never be tied up in the bottom of a ship, but you might have a bad day at school.

You might strike out at bat or—worse—get cut from the team.

A friend might give you the cold shoulder or say something that hurts your feelings.

Your parents might get after you for something that's not your fault.

A teacher might send you into the hall when everyone in the room knows it was Steve who threw the paper airplane.

Your best friends might go to the movies without inviting you.

Someone in your family might get hurt or sick, or might lose his job. Someone close to you might pass away. There are a million things that could come up to discourage you, hurt you, distract you, or threaten your peace of mind.

But when they do, you can still choose what your attitude is going to be! You can choose to be miserable and let it ruin your day. Or—like

> While Joseph Smith was a prisoner in Liberty Jail, the Lord comforted him saying, "My son, peace be unto thy soul; thine adversity and thine afflictions shall be but a small moment; and then, *if thou endure it well*, God shall exalt thee on high" (D&C 121:7–8, emphasis added).
>
> Remember that *your* trials and challenges will eventually pass too. Follow the Lord's counsel and be patient . . . Learn to endure the tough times well.
>
> Trust your Heavenly Father to see that everything works out for your good.

Nephi—you can remember that your Heavenly Father still loves you. You can remember that he is watching over you. You can remember that he will give you the strength to make it through your tough times.

And you can remember that the Lord has promised that as you remain faithful, as you do your best to have a good attitude, he will make your trials and challenges work out for your good (D&C 121:7–8; 122:7).

I used to coach baseball with a man named Jody. We coached great kids but still lost games once in a while. Losing is never fun, and sometimes—after a bad game—the kids would be sitting miserably in the dugout. Jody would always try cheering them up.

"I know how bad you feel," he'd say. "But remember that the sun's still going to come up in the morning."

When my parents were Webelos leaders, they once taught their Scouts how to make homemade ice cream. The kids were all excited and couldn't wait to dive in.

But when it was finished, the boys only took a single taste or two before pulling faces and politely saying they didn't want any more.

My parents were perplexed until they tasted it themselves . . . and discovered that they'd forgotten to add sugar!

Blech!

No wonder no one liked it!

When you make ice cream—or anything else, for that matter—you need to include *all* the ingredients. And those ingredients work together to make something tasty. Even the ones that don't taste so good by themselves.

(By itself, baking soda tastes pretty nasty. But without it, chocolate chip cookies are yuuuuucky!)

Your life is like that. It's the *sum* of all your experiences that makes you what you are. Even the ones that aren't so fun. That's why the Lord said, "*All* things shall work *together* for your good" (D&C 90:24, emphasis added).

And that's good advice for you too. You might be having a bad day, but the sun's going to come up in the morning. There are better times ahead. As the Prophet David said, "weeping may endure for a night, but joy cometh in the morning" (Psalms 30:5).

One of my favorite hymns contains these lines:

> When dark clouds of trouble hang o'er us
> And threaten our peace to destroy,
> *There is hope smiling brightly before us,*
> *And we know that deliv'rance is nigh*;
> ("We Thank Thee O God for a Prophet," *Hymns*, 19,
> emphasis added).

There *will* be tough times ahead. That's part of life, and everyone has them. When your turn comes, don't give up. Keep believing. Keep hoping. Keep praying. Keep your head up and put a smile on your face and a song in your heart.

Remember that the sun will come up again.

And remember that everything—everything—you endure will be for your good.

Jesus faithfully endured great agony in the Garden of Gethsemane.

He endured awful humiliation on the road to Golgotha.

He endured the horrible pain of death on the cross.

Those were each enormous challenges. They were huge trials. But they led to our Lord's greatest triumph and victory.

EVERYONE HAS BAD DAYS NOW AND THEN.

When your turn comes, use these tips to not only survive those tough times but also come out bigger, better, and stronger than ever!

- **PRAY.** When Joseph Smith first went into the woods to pray, he was overwhelmed and almost overpowered by the forces of darkness. But in that moment of despair, Joseph began praying even harder! Prayer will give you the strength to make it through dark times too.

- **FAST.** My tenth-grade seminary teacher called prayer and fasting "the ole one-two punch." Fasting will add power to your prayers, helping you to become even closer to your Heavenly Father. That closeness will supply additional strength for enduring tough trials and challenges.

- **LOOK FOR WAYS TO HELP OTHERS.** When you're going through tough times, your friends or family might be hurting too. Look for ways to help them. I believe that when we reach out to help others through their tough times, the Lord will bless us by helping us through ours too.

- **LOOK FOR SOLUTIONS.** Rather than waste time fretting about how bad things are, try looking for ways to solve the problem. When Nephi broke his bow (1 Nephi 16:18), he didn't waste time sitting around feeling sorry for himself. He got up, made himself a new bow, and went hunting.

- And remember Ammon? After serving King Lamoni for three days, he was watering the king's sheep when mischievous Lamanites came and scattered the flock. The other servants ran for their lives, believing the king would slay them for losing his sheep. Ammon could have run too. But rather than worry, he took action! He got the guys back together and gathered up the sheep!

- When you're faced with a problem, follow Nephi's and Ammon's examples. Look for ways to solve the problem!

- **ASK FOR A BLESSING.** A priesthood blessing can be a powerful tool. Try asking your father, brother, home teacher, neighbor, or bishop. Ask for the strength and peace you need to endure your trials. Ask for the faith to remember that they will work out for your good.

- **COUNT YOUR BLESSINGS.** As bad as things might seem, there are certain to be things you can be thankful for. Learn to focus on those things that are going right in your life, and not on the things that are going wrong.

When I've had problems, I've often used the following chart to help me work things through. Take a look and see if it might help the next time a tough challenge shows up in your life (see chart on next page):

Think of a challenge, problem, or trial that *you're* facing. What is it:

Now think of someone you admire. It can be a family member, a friend, or someone you know at school. Who is it?

Now, how do you think they would handle your particular problem? Would they let it ruin their day? Or would they be like Nephi, being patient, faithful, and courageous as they worked things out?

Would they have a good attitude?

Would they try to learn for it?

(This really is a good way to get yourself working in the right direction . . . so please, *please* give it a try!)

What's one thing you could do today—*right now*—that would help you to solve the problem or make you feel better about it?

Now list one more thing you could do *right now* to make the situation better or easier to deal with. What is it?

Now, don't waste another second! **GO DO IT!**

SIX ⦿ MARSHMALLOWS AND DUM-DUMS
YOU ARE WHAT YOU READ

The campfire snapped and crackled and popped, sending weird shadows dancing through the forest and filling the air with the scent of tangy pine needles. Fourteen-year-old Robbie Jones skewered a plump marshmallow on a stick and held it over the fire.

"It can't be true," he said.

"What can't be true?'

"That you are what you eat." He flexed like a champion weight lifter showing off a sculpted body. "With biceps like these, no way I'm a marshmallow!"

"Well, I think it's true," a Scout named Jordan countered. He turned to a third boy and said, "I saw Robbie sneaking one of Brother Wilson's Twinkies at lunch."

The rest of the troop howled as Robbie blushed.

"No, you watch," Robbie said. "Years from now, little kids will study muscles like mine in school . . ."

"Only if you leave your body to science fiction!"

The Scouts howled again as Robbie's shoulders slumped in defeat.

The troop had spent the day hiking and fishing, and everyone was just starting to wind down before going to bed. As the Scouts joshed and teased one another, Jordan turned to a boy named Hunter, who was sitting on the end of a log.

"What's the matter?" he asked. "You look sad."

Hunter shook his head. "I'm still thinking about what Robbie said . . . about being what you eat."

"Why?"

Hunter sighed, then pulled a handful of Dum-Dums from his pocket.

Everyone howled again, and a couple of boys threw marsh-mallows in Hunter's direction.

I couldn't help grinning. The Scouts were all great kids—all neighbors of mine—and they often invited me along on troop hikes and campouts. I decided to rescue Robbie and Hunter from further persecution.

"What if it's not 'you are what you eat'?" I asked. "What if it's 'you are what you read'?"

I glanced around the campfire. "How many of you would be Hogwarts Wizards?"

A bunch of hands went up around the circle.

"How many of you would be dragon riders?"

Another bunch of hands went up.

"Veggie Vampires?"

More hands.

"Teenage Spies?"

More hands.

"Hobbits? Athletes? Ninjas?"

More hands, more hands, more hands.

And then came the sixty-four dollar question. "If you are what you read," I asked, "how many of you would be Nephi?"

I glanced around the campfire as the boys thought about it.

"How many of you would be Moroni? Or Alma? Or a Stripling Warrior?"

As we talked about being what you read, Hunter began shaking his head again.

"What's wrong with you?" Jordan asked.

"I read my math book," Hunter said.

"Your math book?"

"Yeah . . . I think that's why I've got so many problems!"

The boys were more thoughtful now. And I was too. I wondered if my own Book of Mormon reading would overpower the crime and adventure novels I loved.

And what about you? If you're reading this book, chances are you like to read. (If you're reading this book, you probably like reading to improve and better yourself.) But when it comes right down to it—if you really are what you read—are you a dragon rider or a Stripling Warrior?

Are you a vampire or a valiant Nephite?

Are you a hobbit or an inspired missionary to the Lamanites?

Are you wielding a wand with other young wizards, or brandishing a gleaming sword alongside Captain Moroni?

Don't get me wrong now! I think it's great that you like to read. And I love diving into great novels too. (One of my dreams, in fact, is to write exciting adventure books.)

But . . . are you also devoting time every day to the Book of Mormon?

Nephi read his scriptures, of course. After his family went into the wilderness, in fact, he walked all the way back to Jerusalem—a round trip of about four weeks—to get the brass plates from Laban. (How far would you walk to get a new set of scriptures?)

Not only that, but he actually risked his life to get them. Remember the story? When Laban learned that Nephi and his brothers wanted the plates, he sent his servants to slay them (1 Nephi 3:25). So when Nephi snuck back into the city for one last try, he literally was risking his life. He knew that Laban's men would murder him if they caught him.

Why would he do that?

Why would he risk his life for a pile of dusty old plates?

"The Lord told him to," my friend Ethan said as we discussed it in seminary. (He used a tone that clearly said, *Duh!*)

And yeah, that's a pretty good reason.

But I think there was more to it than that. For one thing, Nephi said that his soul delighted in the scriptures. (See 2 Nephi 4:15.)

Waz that mean?

"He wasn't just reading ten minutes a day, that's for sure," Ethan announced. (His voice still had that irritating *duh* sound to it.) "He wasn't just reading a chapter here or a chapter there."

So what was he doing?

I think Nephi used his scriptures to recharge his spiritual batteries. I think he used them to shape and hone his spiritual muscles, finding the spiritual strength and energy he needed to endure the trials and challenges of his day. (Which certainly came in handy after a long day of dealing with those goofy brothers.)

Think about a bunch of helium balloons. You know, the kind they have at birthday parties? They're bright and cheerful and colorful, bouncing around at the end of their strings. It's like they've got all the energy in the world. If you let go of them, they go soaring into the sky.

But after a day or two, even the brightest balloons begin to deflate. They get wrinkled. They start to sag. Eventually they lose their buoyancy and sink to the ground.

But . . . if you took a minute every day to pump a little fresh helium into them, they'd stay bright and bouncy forever.

Now, you're much the same way. You might one day have an exciting experience that puts you on a "spiritual high," making you feel pretty terrific. You might be so pumped up that you go strutting around like you're Nephi, Moroni, and all two thousand stripling warriors rolled into one magnificent rock-'em, sock-'em, pump-me-up, knock-me-down, super-spiritual-letting-my-spotlight-shine teenager!

But then you have a bad day in school.

Wffft!

It's like you lose a little helium.

Then one of your friends does something that hurts your feelings.

Wffft!

You lose a little more.

One of your teachers piles on a huge homework assignment

when you've already got a ton of math and English to finish.

Wfffft!

Your little brother deletes the ten-page research paper that's due the next day, that cute someone you like asks someone else to the dance, your coach doesn't let you start the game.

Wfffft!

Wfffft!

Wfffft!

I'm going to go out on a limb and guess that you have a cell phone. (If you don't, I'm sure one day you will!)

So what happens if you don't pop that phone into a recharger once in a while? That's right: it quits working.

It's a sad fact, but I think that many people spend more time recharging their phones than they spend recharging their spiritual batteries. But if you don't recharge those spiritual batteries, they will go just as dead.

So what about you? Do you spend as much time recharging your spiritual batteries as you spend charging your cell phone?

Do you need to do a little better?

Man, you're losing helium and you're losing it fast!

Whaddya do?

How do you refill that spiritual helium?

One of the best ways is to read . . . your . . . scriptures!

Why?

Because the scriptures have the power to recharge your spiritual batteries. They have the power to get you over the bumps and snags that make life difficult. They have the power to boost your energy, fan your fire, lift your spirits, and put the spring back in your step.

"FOR MY SOUL DELIGHTETH IN THE SCRIPTURES" (2 NEPHI 4:15).

Now, I know what you're thinking. People have been telling you to "pray and read your scriptures" your whole life. And there are times when plowing through a page of "begats" and "begollies" isn't what you need to fire your engine.

But when you come across one of those verses that seems to be

This past school year I placed this scripture on my desk and tried to apply it every day: "I would that ye should be humble, and be submissive and gentle; easy to be entreated; full of patience and long-suffering; being temperate in all things; being diligent in keeping the commandments of God at all times; asking for whatsoever things ye stand in need, both spiritual and temporal; always returning thanks unto God for whatsoever things ye do receive" (Alma 7:23).

Yes, I still made mistakes. But that verse helped me to remember the direction I wanted to go in my life.

I tried to be more patient.

I tried to be more humble, and more submissive (even to my principal).

It really did make a difference to me, and the same thing can make a difference to you. So find a scripture that will guide you. And then carry it around! Refer to it often. Look at it in the morning and try to think of ways you can apply it during the day. And then look at it again before you go to bed, asking yourself how you did. Decide if there's something different you can do tomorrow!

written just for you, one that gives you the exact boost you need that day, that's fun! That's exciting! And I think that's the sort of thing that got Nephi so excited about his scriptures.

So when Nephi said his soul delighted in the scriptures, I think it's because he was using them to fill in those spiritual voids, using them to pump him up and replenish the energy drained away by spiritual vampires.

The scriptures can recharge your batteries. They can refill your spiritual balloons. They can give you the spiritual energy to run faster than a speeding bishop and to leap tall missionaries in a single bound.

They really can.

How?

Let me give you a few suggestions!

TRY "SKIMMING"

For a change of pace, I often "skim" my scriptures. Rather than reading from cover to cover or from chapter to chapter, I just begin turning pages, reading only those verses I've marked and those notes I've written in the margins. When I need a quick, spiritual "pick-me-up," I'm amazed at how often I'll find exactly what I need within just a few pages.

If your scriptures are new, it might take a while before you have a lot of "energizer" verses marked. But get started! Get a colored pencil and shade in a few of your favorite verses.

And the next time you hear a great scripture in a sacrament meeting or fireside talk, mark it!

If your seminary teacher gives you an insight on a special verse, write a note in the margin!

If you'll start today, it won't be long until you have a good selection of inspirational verses to skim from!

SEARCH FOR SPECIFIC TOPICS

If you're feeling discouraged, try looking up topics such as "hope" and "faith" in the Topical Guide. Then read those scriptures it refers you to.

(I've recently been searching the Book of Mormon for examples of leadership, trying to see how leaders such as Nephi, Ammon, and Captain Moroni inspired and motivated those who followed them.)

You can also search conference talks, church magazines, and study guides on lds.org for specific issues you might be dealing with. Look especially for verses the speakers refer to, then mark them in your scriptures.

And don't be afraid to write your own thoughts, feelings, and insights in the margins. This is a great way to personalize your scriptures.

INSERT CONFERENCE TALKS AND QUOTES IN YOUR SCRIPTURES

When a speaker discusses a scripture during general conference, clip his talk from the *Ensign* (or print in from lds .org). Then place it in your scriptures. (Sometimes I'll include the whole article, and sometimes I'll just clip the paragraph or two that pertains to that scripture.) This will help you remember certain points months or even years later.

In my Book of Mormon I have a talk by Elder Boyd K. Packer called "Balm of Gilead." I clipped it from the November issue of the *Ensign* in 1987. (That means it's been in my scriptures for more than twenty years!)

I had an incredible experience with this just today. I'd been feeling bad about a couple of things, and I'd told myself that I needed to have a good prayer . . . that I really needed to ask my Heavenly Father for help. But before I did, I happened to be skimming my scriptures and by Acts 28:5 (where Paul shakes off the snake that had bitten him) I found part of a talk I'd once heard, and then placed in my scriptures. The quote went like this: "When someone does something that hurts you, shake it off! Don't let it ruin your day. Don't let their poisonous spirit hurt you.

"Maybe someone's rejected you, or been negative toward you, or criticized you. And maybe you've let those 'zingers' get you down."

And man, that's exactly what had happened to me. I couldn't have phrased my problem any better.

And the talk went on, "It's time to 'shake it off!' Wash away the poison and keep your inner self fresh and clean.

"When someone talks negatively about you, trying to make you look bad, their words can really sting. But shake them off. Remember that God is in control, and that he will take care of you."

Those words were exactly what I needed to hear. And when I finally knelt down to talk with my Heavenly Father, I didn't ask for help. Instead, I said thanks . . . thanks for answering my prayer (before I'd even prayed).

WRITE YOUR OWN INTERPRETATION IN THE MARGINS

I do this all the time. In the margin beside Isaiah 60:1 ("Arise, shine; for thy light is come . . ."), I wrote, "I think Isaiah is saying, 'Get up from the couch! Shake off that discouragement! Get your enthusiasm back! Laugh! Run! Play a game! Get the spark back in your life!'"

And next to 2 Nephi 1:23 ("Awake, my sons; put on the armor of righteousness. Shake off the chains with which ye are bound, and come forth out of obscurity, and arise from the dust . . .") I wrote, "Be happy! Don't let the little things get you down! Get up, put a smile on your face, and get back to work!"

When you're really paying attention in church, or during general conference, firesides, and seminary, you'll often hear thoughts and ideas you can use.

"LINK" OR CROSS-REFERENCE YOUR FAVORITE STORIES AND TOPICS

When Lehi died, I was impressed with how Nephi chose to stay positive, counting his blessings and focusing on those things going right in his life instead of those things going wrong: "Awake, my soul!" he wrote. "Rejoice, O my heart" (2 Nephi 4:28).

In the margin beside that verse, I wrote down the references to these other "choose-to-be-happy" verses:

Romans 12:2 ("Be ye transformed by the renewing of your mind.")

Isaiah 60:1 ("Arise, shine; for thy light is come.")

I've always thought that Ammon was one of the world's most unstoppable optimists. After all, when the sheep were scattered and everyone thought the king would kill them all, Ammon's "heart was swollen within him with joy" (Alma 17:29).

The Apostle Paul was the same way. In the middle of a ferocious storm that was shaking his little ship to pieces, Paul said to his friends, "And now I exhort you to be of good cheer"! (Acts 27:22.)

What great attitudes! I have those stories cross-referenced with Nephi's attitude in 2 Nephi 4:28.

1 Peter 1:13 ("Gird up the loins of your mind.")

Ephesians 4:23 ("Be renewed in the spirit of your mind.")

Acts 27:22 ("And now I exhort you to be of good cheer.")

Ezekial 18:32 ("Wherefore turn yourselves, and live ye.")

Psalms 40:3 ("And he hath put a new song in my mouth.")

WRITE DOWN INSIGHTS AND EXPLANATIONS IN THE MARGINS

When I first read the Book of Mormon, I wondered why the Lord wouldn't let Lehi's family build fires while they traveled through the wilderness. (See 1 Nephi 17:12.)

Not even to cook with!

Instead, he made the food "sweet," so they didn't have to cook it.

I remember shaking my head, wondering what that was all about.

But it all made sense when my seminary teacher pointed out that the wilderness was full of thieves, robbers, and bandits who would have been attracted by the smoke and flames of large cooking fires (and who would have given the family one more problem to deal with).

So, yeah, I wrote that down in the margin.

And beside 1 Nephi 3:7 ("I will go and do the things which the Lord hath commanded") I wrote: "What faith it takes to say, 'I will go and do . . .' When Nephi said that, he had no idea the Lord would send him back to Jerusalem; that he'd ask him to slay Laban; and that he'd ask him to build a ship. But Nephi was true to his word. No matter what the Lord asked, Nephi agreed to do it."

When you're reading your seminary manual or listening to Sunday School talks and lessons you'll often find thoughts and insights that will make the scriptures more clear and interesting.

Write them down!

"LIKEN" THE SCRIPTURES TO YOURSELF

Nephi wrote that he "likened" the scriptures to himself. (See 1 Nephi 19:23.)

Waz that mean?

Simply that when he read the scriptures, he looked for ways to apply them to his own life. When Laman and Lemuel began whining about going after the brass plates, for instance, Nephi used stories from the scriptures to motivate and encourage them.

"Let us be strong like unto Moses" he once told them, "for he truly spake unto the waters of the Red Sea and they divided hither and thither, and our fathers came through, out of captivity, on dry ground, and the armies of Pharaoh did follow and were drowned in the waters of the Red Sea" (1 Nephi 4:2).

(I love that strategy! Nephi was saying, "Hey, guys, Moses took on Pharaoh's entire army . . . we're only taking on a measly fifty guys!")

Later, when Laman and Lemuel began fussing about having to help Nephi build a ship, Nephi told them even more stories about Moses, reminding them of all the fantastic things the ancient prophet accomplished:

> I don't think it's a coincidence that Nephi used Moses as an example. After all, Moses and his people were traveling through the wilderness, just as Nephi's family was doing.
>
> Just as Nephi used Moses as a great example, we can use Nephi's example and teachings to help us in our lives.

- He led the children of Israel out of bondage (1 Nephi 17:23).
- He parted the Red Sea for them (1 Nephi 17:26).
- When the people ran out of water, Moses smote a rock, which then produced water (1 Nephi 17:29).
- He led the people to the land of promise (1 Nephi 17:42).

Nephi also reminded his brothers how the Lord helped his people through their trials:

- When they ran out of food in the wilderness, the Lord supplied them with manna (1 Nephi 17:28).
- The Lord went before them, leading them by day and giving them light by night (1 Nephi 17:30).

One of my favorite ways to liken the scriptures to myself is to find a verse that really strikes me. Then I write it on a card and carry it with me, and I really do try to apply it.

I've already mentioned one of these, but here's another one that I often carry in my pocket: "Remember faith, virtue, knowledge, temperance, patience, brotherly kindness, godliness, charity, humility, diligence" (D&C 4:6).

Boy, doesn't that just about cover every situation that might come up in your day?

KEEP READING YOUR SCRIPTURES . . . AGAIN AND AGAIN

After they went into the wilderness, Lehi's family needed directions. (Laman and Lemuel were lost from the start, but that's a different story.) But the Lord was ready for that. He prepared a ball of "curious workmanship" that acted like a compass.

Well, that's the way it worked most of the time.

Unlike a Boy Scout compass, the Liahona (as Alma called it) only worked when the family was living righteously.

Sounds good, huh?

Live the commandments, the compass works. Get a little rowdy and you're on . . . your . . . own.

And that wasn't all. There was writing on the compass needles that miraculously changed from time to time, offering additional suggestions and guidance.

And they weren't weird, cryptic clues like the ones in

> When I was a missionary in the MTC, our scripture teacher told us that he'd read Isaiah more than one hundred times.
>
> "The first twenty or thirty times, I didn't get it at all," he said. "The next forty or fifty times, it started to make a little sense."
>
> His eyes twinkled. "And now it's the most exciting book I've ever read!"

the National Treasure and Da Vinci Code movies. They were (as Nephi put it) "plain to be read" (1 Nephi 16:29).

Now that's a great story. But I don't think Nephi was simply giving us interesting details about his journey in the wilderness. There was a point to his story. The question is, what does it have to do with you?

I'm so glad you asked!

When I read the scriptures, there are times when certain verses jump out at me, affecting me like never before. Even verses I've read many, many times will suddenly take on new meaning.

Nephi said that his soul delighted in the scriptures. Waz that mean?

Do you think he was reading just ten minutes a day?

Think he was reading to get it over with?

Or was he really reading them, hunting and searching for those little treasures that would bless and energize him?

Is there anything you can learn from his example?

Sometimes I'll read a scripture and it will be like reading it for the first time. It will suddenly relate to something going on in my life and take on a whole new meaning. And in that way, I think, the the scriptures change, much like the spindles changed in the Liahona.

That's one reason you should read the Book of Mormon again and again . . . and again.

Remember those helium balloons. Even if you're the most spiritually-charged teenager on the planet, the bumps and grinds of daily life can easily drain your spiritual energy.

But if you take a few minutes every day to recharge those batteries you can maintain and even strengthen your spirit. You can be sure that you have the spiritual energy you need . . . when you need it!

And one of the best, easiest, most effective ways to do that is to read . . . your . . . scriptures.

If you're not already reading them, start today! Read them!

And read them every day!

SEVEN
"GOTTA GET TO THE GAME!"
SAYING PRAYERS THAT CONNECT

"Hello, Brother Barker? This is Devin Marshall . . ."

"Well, hi, Devin!" I said, surprised to hear his voice. "What's going on—"

"Are you really busy right now?"

"No, not really," I said. "Why? Is something wrong—"

"I've got a soccer game in twenty minutes. My mom just called and she's not going to be home in time to take me. I've got to be there and I don't know what to do."

I could hear the urgency in Devin's voice, and he was almost pleading as he asked, "Is there any chance you could drive me to my game?"

"Yeah, not a problem," I said. "I'll be right over."

Okay, I thought as I drove to Devin's house, picturing the route to the soccer complex. *Game starts in twenty—well, about fifteen minutes now . . . yeah, we can make it . . .*

Devin lived just around the corner from me. His father was a colonel in the National Guard and had been in Afghanistan for the past four months. Fourteen years old, Devin was the oldest child in the Marshall family, and I knew he was worried about his father being gone . . . not to mention being in a war zone.

"Hey, I know I'm not your home teacher or anything," I'd once told him. "But I want to help. If I can ever do anything for you—if you ever need anything—please don't hesitate to ask."

"Okay," Devin had said. But until now he'd never taken me up on the offer.

"Thanks so much," he said when he jumped into my truck. "You just saved my life."

"Not a problem," I said. "I'm actually glad you called."

And I was. I wasn't just making empty promises when I'd offered to help. And I love going to ball games. I often take books I'm working on with me and—sitting on the sidelines—I usually get more done than when I'm sitting at my desk at home.

Besides, I like feeling helpful. And needed. I really was glad that when the chips were down and Devin needed help, he'd thought of me.

Devin had worried about calling me, worried that he was imposing, or taking advantage of me. But I was glad he'd asked! It made me feel good being able to help.

And you know what? I believe that our Heavenly Father is excited when we go to him for help too.

Some time after Nephi's family went into the wilderness, his father Lehi had a fantastic dream. He saw buildings, trees, crowds of people, mists of darkness, and each of his sons. A few days

Because I'm a school teacher, I'm used to having students ask me for help with their assignments. Sometimes—especially after a fantastic lesson—I can't help wondering, Hey! Were you listening to anything I said?

But I always try to remind myself, "Hey! There's a real, live kid here . . . a kid who's actually trying to learn this stuff! How awesome is that!"

And that attitude gets me excited to help.

I sincerely believe that our Heavenly Father is excited when we approach him in prayer. I believe he's thinking something like, "Wow! There's a real, live son or daughter who needs my help!" or "I'm so glad they've come to me!"

I believe he loves being asked for help. I believe he loves being able to "team up" with us, helping us to create miracles in our lives. And many times he's just waiting for us to ask!

later, Nephi found his brothers talking it over, wondering what the strange dream meant.

Nephi asked them, "Have ye inquired of the Lord?" (1 Nephi 15:8.)

Now, I'm sure you've heard that story before. But I want you to think about something. You see, Nephi wasn't just asking an idle question. He'd wanted to know the meaning of Lehi's dream too. And so he'd inquired, asking the Lord to explain it to him.

The result was an amazing revelation. An angel appeared to Nephi, talking with him like a good friend. The angel took Nephi on a kind of journey, showing him spectacular things, answering his questions, and explaining what Lehi's dream was all about.

"Ask, and it shall be given you; seek, and ye shall find; knock, and it shall be opened unto you" (Matt 7:7).

Have you ever wondered what sort of things you should pray about?

Amulek said to "cry unto [your Heavenly Father] when ye are in your fields, yea over all your flocks.

"Cry unto him in your houses, yea, over all your household, both morning, mid-day, and evening.

"Cry unto him over the crops of your fields, that ye may prosper in them.

"Cry over the flocks of your fields, that they may increase" (Alma 34:20–21, 24–25).

Alma said to ask "for whatsoever things ye stand in need, both spiritual *and* temporal" (Alma 7:23, emphasis added).

I think Alma's making things pretty clear: Do you need something? Anything? Just ask!

That had to have been an awesome experience. And afterward Nephi surely felt razzled, dazzled, and overwhelmed by it all.

And that was when he came across his brothers. So when Nephi asked if they'd inquired of the Lord, what he was really saying was, "Holy cow, guys . . . you gotta question? Go ask! 'Cause man, I just did that and boy did I ever get an answer!"

And when his slow-to-believe brothers asked what he was talking about, I can just picture Nephi nodding and saying, "Guys, you gotta trust me on this . . . the Lord's just waiting for you to ask and brother, the answer is fan-tas-tic!"

There's a lot we can learn from that story. But the point I want to make is this: the Lord wanted to bless Nephi. He wanted to answer his questions. But notice that he didn't simply appear to Nephi out of the blue.

He waited for Nephi to ask!

And it wasn't just Nephi. When you read Lehi's dream (1 Nephi 8), you learn that Lehi started out walking through a dreary wilderness. That wasn't a whole lot of fun, and after several hours he began to pray for help.

When the Lord asked Nephi to build a ship, he didn't hand him a how-to-build-it manual and say, "Okay, here's everything you need to know." Remember that Nephi had never built a ship before, and this one wasn't going to be built "after the manner of men" anyway. But the Lord promised to show him exactly what he needed to do. (See 1 Nephi 17:8, and 1 Nephi 18:1–3.)

Instead, he gave Nephi enough information to get started, then chipped in additional instructions from time to time. And Nephi went to "pray oft" as various questions, problems, and concerns came up.

Now, the Lord's not going to give you all the answers you need all at once either. Instead he'll teach you bit by bit, line upon line, precept upon precept.

So as things change and new situations come up in your life, you need to be like Nephi and "pray oft." That's why it's so important to keep your communication lines open, praying often, seeking guidance for new and changing challenges.

And that's when an angel showed up to deliver him.

Now, I think something crucial happened right there. Did you catch it?

The Lord wanted to talk to Lehi. But he waited for Lehi to ask!

Now let's jump forward a few thousand years. We're in New York now, where a fourteen-year-old boy named Joseph Smith is wondering which church to join. And you know, I believe the Lord wanted to talk to Joseph Smith. He was waiting to talk to Joseph Smith. But he didn't just appear to Joseph out of the blue.

He waited for Joseph to ask.

A couple of years went by, and Joseph began to wonder how he stood with the Lord. So once again he began to pray. And he received an incredible visit from the Angel Moroni.

Are you seeing a pattern yet?

Moroni wanted to talk to Joseph Smith.

But he waited for Joseph to ask!

A few years later, Joseph was translating the plates with Oliver Cowdery. They came across a reference to baptism, and not quite understanding it they went into the woods to pray. And received a visit from John the Baptist.

Yes, I sincerely believe that John the Baptist wanted to talk to Joseph and Oliver. But he waited for them to ask!

We could go on and on. But if you take a minute to think about it, you'll notice that many of the most important and dramatic visions and revelations of the restored Church came about because someone asked a question! And the point I'm trying to make is this: What

> President Thomas S. Monson has said that prayer can "solve more problems, alleviate more suffering, prevent more transgression, and bring about greater peace and contentment in the human soul than could be obtained in any other way" ("Come unto Him in Prayer and Faith," *Ensign*, March 2009, 4–9).

great things do you think the Lord wants to tell you . . . things that he's just waiting for you to ask for?

You see, your Heavenly Father has all kinds of gifts and blessings that he's reserved just for you. Don't let them sit around in some heavenly box gathering heavenly dust!

Ask for them!

Have you got a question about something?

Ask!

Need a friend?

Ask!

Need a word of encouragement, the strength to endure a difficult time, a bit of comfort when things aren't working out?

Ask!

Ask!

Ask!

President Marion G. Romney once said, "As there is no limitation as to *when* we should pray, so there seems to be no limitation as to *where* we should pray or *what we should pray about*" (Conference Report, Oct. 1944, 55, emphasis added).

There have been times when I've been in tight spots, times when I've needed help and needed it bad. I was once flying a small plane, for instance, and had to make an emergency landing.

Another time I was on a cross-country ski trip when we were hit by an avalanche.

And once I was driving down a backcountry road in the rain when I came across a bad accident. Those were all real emergencies, and when I prayed for help, I prayed what Enos might have called "mighty prayers." (See Enos 4.)

And there have been times when I've needed things that might have seemed a little silly. There was a time when I was lonely and needed a friend. That wasn't nearly as critical as being in an airplane that was falling out of the sky (or as scary as trying to outski an avalanche). But that made it even more touching that my Heavenly Father understood my needs and answered my prayers.

WHEN JOSEPH SMITH WAS FOURTEEN, HE WAS WONDERING

which church he should join. And one day he happened to read James 1:5: "If any of you lack wisdom, let him ask of God, that giveth to all men liberally, and upbraideth not; and it shall be given him."

I'm sure you've read that verse before, but let's break it down and analyze what it's really saying.

"If any of you . . ."

This scripture doesn't just apply to bishops, or stake presidents, or general authorities. It applies to me. It applies to you. It applies to everyone.

". . . lack wisdom . . ."

If you ever feel lost, or uncertain; if you ever have questions; if you ever have problems you just don't know how to handle . . .

". . . let him ask of God . . ."

Who knows "all things from the beginning" (1 Nephi 9:6), who knows exactly what you're feeling and exactly what you're going through, and who knows the answer to every problem you have . . . long before you even have the problem!

". . . that giveth to all men liberally . . ."

Liberally means generously. You see, the Lord doesn't stockpile his blessings. He doesn't put them aside or lock them up or save them for special occasions. No, he gives them now, he gives them often, and he gives them generously.

". . . and upbraideth not . . ."

The Lord won't get mad at you for asking. He won't lecture you for asking. He won't criticize you and he won't get after you. You don't have to worry about him saying "Hey! If you'd been paying attention in Sunday School you'd already know this!"

". . . and it shall be given him."

Prayer worked for Lehi. It worked for Nephi. It worked for Joseph Smith and it will work for you.

President Thomas S. Monson once said, "Perhaps there has never been a time when we had greater need to pray. . . . It is through earnest and heartfelt prayer that we can receive the needed blessings and the support required to make our way in this sometimes difficult and challenging journey we call mortality"("Three Goals to Guide You," *Ensign*, Nov. 2007, 118–21).

I teach at a junior high school where we have a great track-and-field program. But this past season a weird flu bug was going around, causing a lot of kids to miss school.

Not only that, but we had a really wet, cold, drizzly spring. On the day of our first track meet, a lot of the kids weren't feeling very well. (They probably should have all stayed home in bed, but no one wanted to miss the action!)

Anyway, because so many of the kids were sick, they all got together before the meet and had a team prayer.

"Really?" I asked when a young man named Keith told me

I have a young friend named Josh who was a student in my geometry class. Toward the end of the year he began coming to class looking quiet, anxious, and withdrawn. One day I asked him, "Are you okay?"

"Yeah," he said. But then he added: "I'm worried about all the end-of-year tests we have coming up."

But a day or two later—on the actual day of the dreaded state math test—he came to class looking relaxed, refreshed, and happy.

"Hey, Josh," I said, "you're looking chipper today."

"Yeah," he said, giving me a happy knuckle bump. "My dad gave me a priesthood blessing this morning."

"Really? Just for this test?"

"Yeah . . . this and biology."

I was impressed . . . both that Josh was so concerned about his scores, and that he felt comfortable enough to ask his father for a blessing.

Josh earned outstanding scores that week, both in geometry and biology. Imagine what great blessings the Lord has reserved for you too . . . blessings that he's just waiting for you to ask for!

about it. After all, prayers aren't always encouraged at school events. And not all the kids were members of the Church.

"As long as there are tests, there will be prayer in school." (Author unknown)

"Oh, yeah," Keith said. "It was right before the meet. Most of us weren't feeling well, and some of the kids were really, really sick. So we got together behind the bleachers and had a prayer."

He gave me a grin. "We weren't praying that we'd win . . . we were just praying that everyone would just be able to do their best and run as well as they could."

"Wow," I said. "Whose idea was that?"

"Amanda Kelly's."

Ah! I thought. That figured. Amanda was in my geometry class, and organizing a team prayer was just the sort of thing she'd do. I already knew of a time when some of the kids were preparing for a tough AP English test. They'd all worked hard to be ready, but many of them were still nervous.

"So we all got together and had a prayer," Amanda told me.

"Even the kids who aren't LDS?"

Amanda gave me a look that told me I was being silly to ask.

"Of course! We just told everyone that we were going to meet in Ms. Smith's room for a prayer before the test," she said. "And everyone who wanted to come was welcome."

"And a lot of people came?"

Amanda beamed.

"Everyone came!" she said. "Every . . . single . . . person."

"Who offered the prayer?"

"I was going to," she said. "But then David Roring volunteered."

Wow, I thought.

I was proud of Amanda for doing that. I was proud of all the kids. I was excited they were comfortable enough to be part of a group prayer. And I was impressed that those kids who were

Okay, this is a silly story, but I can't resist! When I was in high school I once went camping with my friend Ethan. We'd been talking about Bigfoot (if you ever spend time with me you usually end up hearing stories about Bigfoot), and we wondered if there were any in the forest we were camping in.

During the night, Ethan was walking along a dark, spooky trail. It was a little bit scary, and after a few minutes he began to pray.

"Heavenly Father," he prayed, "I'd like to see a Bigfoot . . . I really would like to see a Bigfoot."

But then—as a spooky breeze rustled the crisp aspen leaves—he began praying more earnestly: "But not right now . . . please, please, please not right now!"

members of the Church were able to set such a good example for their friends.

I have a testimony that the Lord watches over us. And that he guides us. And that many times he gives us blessings that we haven't asked for, and that we might not even realize that we need.

But I also believe there are times when he wants us to ask.

Remember that when the Lord restored his Church to the earth, he didn't give the prophet Joseph all the answers all at once. Instead, he gave him just enough information to get started. But then he was there to help as new situations and challenges cropped up.

The Lord isn't going to give you the answers to your problems all at once either. That's why you need to stay close, keeping in touch, and asking for help as you need it.

The question is, do your prayers make it all the way to heaven?

Or do they just bounce off the ceiling?

Take a minute to look over the checkup below:

President Thomas S. Monson once said, "Through personal prayer, through family prayer, by trusting in God with faith, nothing wavering, we can call down to our rescue His mighty power. His call to us is as it has ever been: 'Come unto me'" (Matthew 11:28) ("Come unto Him in Prayer and Faith," *Ensign*, March 2009, 4–9).

PRAYER CHECKUP

(Circle the answer that best describes you)

When I pray, I always:

	ABSOLUTELY!			NOT SO MUCH!	
First prepare myself, making sure my heart and mind are in tune with the Spirit	1	2	3	4	5
Take time to meditate and ponder those things I'm going to pray about	1	2	3	4	5
Pray as if I'm really *talking* with my Heavenly Father	1	2	3	4	5
Pray often (not just when I have problems)	1	2	3	4	5
Take time to thank the Lord for the help and blessings I receive	1	2	3	4	5
Wait patiently for answers	1	2	3	4	5
Have faith the Lord will hear and answer my prayers	1	2	3	4	5
Do my best to do my part to receive the blessings I'm asking for	1	2	3	4	5

As you look over your answers, do you see anything you can improve on? What is it?

_____

_____

What could you do to earn a better score in that area?

_____

_____

Is there another item you could be better at? Which one?

_____

_____

What could you start doing today to be better at that?

_____

_____

If there's one thing you could do today to improve the quality and power of your personal prayers, what would it be?

_____

_____

Now . . . what are you waiting for? Go do it!

The Lord told Joseph Smith to "pray always." Consider these tips and suggestions as you become closer to your Heavenly Father through sincere, heartfelt prayer:

Once, after an argument with his wife Emma, Joseph Smith was unable to translate the plates. Finally, after apologizing to Emma and making peace with her, Joseph was again able to translate as usual. Is there anything you need to do to prepare your heart and mind for prayer? What is it?

_____

Nephi often went into the mountains to pray (1 Nephi 18:3), and Joseph Smith chose a grove of woods for his first prayer (JS-History 1:14). Why do you suppose they did that?

_____

If you need to offer an extra special prayer, is there a secluded place you could go? Where is it?

_____

Lehi prayed with "all his heart" (1 Nephi 1:5), and Alma "poured out his whole soul to God" (Mosiah 26:14). If a prophet is required to pour out his whole soul, what does that say about our prayers?

_____

President Gordon B. Hinckley once said, "The trouble with most of our prayers is that we give them as if we were picking up the telephone and ordering groceries—we place our order and hang up. We need to meditate, contemplate, [and] think of what we are praying about" (_Teachings of Gordon B. Hinckley_, [Salt Lake City: Deseret Book, 1997], 469).

What can you do to be sure _you're_ not offering "grocery list" prayers?

_____

Nephi, Enos, Alma, and others described offering "mighty" prayers (2 Nephi 4:24, Enos 4, Alma 8:10, 3 Nephi 27:1). What do you suppose that means?

_____

Have you ever offered a "mighty" prayer? Could you? What would a "mighty" prayer be like?

_____

President Thomas S. Monson once said, "If any of us has been slow to hearken to the counsel to pray always, there is no finer hour to begin than now" ("Come unto Him in Prayer and Faith," *Ensign*, March 2009, 4–9).

How does President Monson's invitation apply to you?

_____

_____

Alma said to pray for "whatsoever thing ye stand in need, both spiritual *and* temporal" (Alma 7:23, emphasis added). He's emphasizing that the Lord will bless us with anything we need, not just things relating to church.

Are there things in your life you could be praying for, but haven't?

What are they?

_____

_____

President Thomas S. Monson told of a frazzled man who helped people with unsolved problems. He placed a sign on his desk that said, "Have you tried prayer?" ("Come unto Him in Prayer and Faith," *Ensign*, March 2009, 4–9).

When you have problems, are you quick to try prayer?

Where would you place yourself on the number line:

Not so much   **Always**

|------------------0------------------|

Where would your Father in Heaven like you to be?

(What can you do better?)

_____

_____

Nephi, Joseph Smith, and Joseph F. Smith each "pondered" and "meditated" as they prayed (1 Nephi 11:1; D&C 76:19; D&C 138:1).

Do you include pondering and mediating with your prayers?

How could you do better?

_____

_____

Prayer is one of the most important blessings the Lord has given us. Through prayer you can receive help with many of the questions and challenges that arise in your life.

Through prayer you can strengthen your testimony and become closer to your Father in Heaven. Through prayer you can receive the strength, guidance, and comfort you need to make it through every challenge you face.

So take the time to pray.

Take the time to pray often.

Remember that your Heavenly Father will hear your prayers. And that he knows all the answers. And that he will answer.

"For every one that asketh receiveth; and he that seeketh findeth; and to him that knocketh it knocketh it shall be opened" (Matthew 7:8).

Most of all, remember the words of the Lord who said, "Pray always, and I will pour out my Spirit upon you, and great shall be your joy" (D&C 19:38).

EIGHT ⊙⊙⊙ CAN'T HANG OUT . . . GOTTA BUILD A SHIP

WHEN IT'S YOUR TURN TO "DO AS THE LORD COMMANDED"

Cassie Hill walked into my classroom with a look of disbelief.

"Guess what happened to me last night!"

"You won your soccer game?"

"Well, yeah . . . but I mean after that."

"Give me a hint."

"I had an interview with my bishop; he called me to be president of the Mia Maids!"

"Hey, Cassie, good for you! That's—"

I was going to say "awesome," but then I saw the look in her eyes.

"What . . . it's not so awesome?"

"Well, it is. But I've never been in charge of anything before."

"And you're worried?"

She nodded.

"What did you say to the bishop?"

"I said yes, but . . . but what if I can't do it? What if"—her eyes became misty—"what if I'm just awful?"

I didn't think Cassie could be awful at anything. But I understood how she was feeling. And I was excited when she came in a few days later beaming like a little kid on Christmas morning.

"We had our first presidency meeting last night," she told me. "And it was so much fun!"

She told me that she'd had a long talk with her advisors, and her counselors, who all promised to give her all the help she needed. And being president of the Mia Maids turned out to be a fantastic experience, one that filled her with enthusiasm and confidence.

One of the most exciting things about the Restored Church is that the Lord gives important jobs and responsibilities to "ordinary" people. And we're not just talking about adults. We're talking about young people too. We're talking about young people like you.

Seriously!

Like Cassie, you might be called to be president of your class or quorum. You might be called to be a counselor. You might be called to serve on a committee, give a talk, be a home teacher, or fellowship someone in the ward.

The possibilities are endless.

And the day might come when—like Cassie—the Lord gives you more than you think you're able to handle. And that's when you need to remember Nephi.

Nephi?

Oh, yeah!

Remember when the Lord asked Nephi and his brothers to get the brass plates from Laban? That seemed like an impossible task. Laman and Lemuel were both certain that it couldn't be done. And after the brothers tried—and failed—twice, Nephi didn't even know how they were ever going to do it.

"If it so be that the children of men keep the commandments of God he doth nourish them, and strengthen them, and provide means whereby they can accomplish the thing which he has commanded them" (1 Nephi 17:3).

But—and here's the key—Nephi knew that the Lord knew how. And he knew that the Lord would help them get the job done.

And the Lord did too. He delivered Laban into Nephi's hands. He helped Nephi to convince Laban's servant Zoram that he—Nephi—was actually Laban, so that Zoram would give him the plates.

That wasn't the only time the Lord stepped in to help. When the family reached the ocean, the Lord told Nephi to build a ship.

A ship.

Just think about that for a second. The Lord wasn't asking Nephi to do something simple like give a talk in sacrament meeting or pass fliers around the ward.

He was asking him to build a ship!

And not just some Huckleberry Finn-kinda raft, either. Nephi had to build a ship big enough to carry the whole family—and their belongings—and strong enough to withstand a trip across the ocean.

When I was your age and in seminary, my friend Ethan made a list of things Nephi could have said about that chore. A few of them went like this:

- "I'd love to, Lord, but shoot . . . I left all my tools back in Jerusalem."
- "A ship! Suuuuure! Lemme just run down to the hardware store and—wait . . . there isn't a hardware store!"
- "Hey! Do I look like I got an A in Shipbuilding?"
- "A ship? This is like a joke, right?"
- "Hey, not a problem! Just show me where to plug in my power saw."
- "Build a ship? Okay . . . but couldn't you just part the sea like you did for Moses?"
- "Hey, sounds like fun! But first, uh, I'm gonna need a buncha hammers, a couple saws, a gajillion nails, and a whole tub full of Super Glue . . ."
- "Yeah, I'll build a ship . . . then next week we could build a rocket and fly to the moon too!"

Nephi knew that the Lord provides ways for people to keep his commandments. And he gave us plenty of examples. When Lehi and his family went into the wilderness, for instance, the Lord told them not to build fires . . . not even to cook with.

"No fires?" my friend Ethan asked our seminary teacher. "That was kinda harsh, wasn't it?"

"You need to remember there were robbers in the wilderness," Brother Sanders explained. "There were thieves, outlaws, bandits . . . and big campfires would have brought them all running."

"Oh, yeah, well," Ethan said. "I knew that . . ."

Anyway, the Lord made the family's meat sweet, so that it didn't need to be cooked (1 Nephi 17:12). In that way, the Lord truly was helping the family to live as he commanded.

You need to know that the Lord will be there to help you live his commandments too.

Yeah, there are a lot of things Nephi could have said. But he didn't.

He didn't even ask for tools.

Instead, he simply asked where he might find ore to make all the tools he was going to need.

And there, I think, is one of the great lessons from the life of Nephi. You see, Nephi knew that the Lord wasn't going to hand everything to him on a silver platter. He knew everything wasn't always going to be easy. He knew from the beginning there was going to be some work involved.

And he didn't waste any time worrying about how hard it was going to be. He didn't worry about the fact that he'd never built a ship. He knew that as long as he did his part, the Lord would give him all the help he needed.

The question is, how does any of this apply to you? Chances are, the Lord's never going to ask you to build a ship. (Can you imagine taking a note like this one to the principal's office?)

FROM THE OFFICE OF THE CHURCH

Please excuse Emily from school this week . . . The Lord needs her to build a ship.

Thank you for understanding.

But one day you might be asked to give a talk in sacrament meeting. You might be called to be a camp leader. You might be asked to organize a service project. You might be asked to take charge of the next combined activity.

Who knows?

You might be called to any one of the assignments your Heavenly Father has reserved for the youth of the Church.

And you might be called to do something that forces you out of your comfort zone. Something that you don't feel comfortable with. Something you don't think you have the skills for.

And when that happens, will you have the confidence you'll need to succeed? Will you be able to take on your assignments with excitement and enthusiasm, trusting your Heavenly Father to be there when you need him?

If you have any doubts, remember Nephi. He didn't worry about how he was going to get the plates, or how in the world he was ever going to build a ship. When the Lord asked him to go to work he immediately said, "Yes, sir!"

And then he tore into the work knowing that as long as he did his part, the Lord would do his.

LET'S TAKE A LOOK AT YOUR ATTITUDE TOWARD DIFFICULT,

unusual, or unpleasant assignments. Read the following statements and decide which one best describes you!

When I'm asked to do something I . . .

Say yes, no matter what it is. (And then I actually do it!)	**10 POINTS**
Say yes, even if I don't really want to do it.	**9 POINTS**
Say yes, but then whine about having to do it.	**8 POINTS**
Say yes, figuring I can find a way to get out of it later.	**7 POINTS**
Say yes, even though I have no intention of actually doing anything.	**6 POINTS**
Say yes, but immediately begin thinking of excuses to get out of it.	**5 POINTS**
Ask for time to "think about it."	**4 POINTS**
Say no before I even hear what's involved.	**3 POINTS**
Say no but then whine about never being included in things.	**2 POINTS**

I'm not really going to ask you for your score. But I'm sure you get the point.

And remember this: as you grow and progress in the Church, you're sure to be given assignments from time to time. And some of them might seem difficult. When those times come, remember Nephi. Remember his example. And remember that the Lord will prepare a way for you to complete whatever he asks you to do.

There was a time when Jesus was teaching in the desert. When it became late and the people became hungry, Jesus took five loaves of bread and a couple of fish and had his disciples pass them out (Matthew 14:13–21).

Five loaves of bread?

Two little fish?

For five thousand people?

Yes! Those few loaves and fish fed five thousand people . . . and there were twelve baskets of food left over!

Just as the Lord magnified those loaves and fishes, he can magnify aspects of your life too. He can magnify your talents, your skills, your abilities, your time, and your strengths in order to do the jobs he's asked you to.

This past summer I was asked to give a talk at a fireside. I had a great idea for a talk, and I put a lot of time into it. I had funny stories, a couple of terrific quotes and scriptures, and one amazing experience that I knew would keep everyone spellbound.

But as I was visiting with some of the youth before we began, I learned that the ward had recently gone through a terrible experience. And just like that I realized that my talk wasn't going to work.

Picture that! The kids were filing into the chapel . . . and I didn't have a talk!

I began to pray, pleading with my Heavenly Father for help. A young woman welcomed everyone to the fireside, and I still didn't know what I was going to do.

We sang a song.

A young man offered a prayer.

I still didn't know what I was going to say.

And then they were introducing me, thanking me for driving more than a hundred miles to speak to them.

And I still didn't know what I was going to say.

As I walked up to the podium, a thought came to me.

Just talk . . .

Just talk? Waz that mean?

I looked out over the audience and the thought came again: Just . . . talk.

When the Lord told Moses to go before Pharaoh, Moses didn't think he could do it. He didn't think he had the ability to confront the most powerful man in Egypt (Exodus 3).

But the Lord was patient. He said, "Moses, tell me what you're holding in your hand there."

"It's a walking stick, Lord."

"Throw it down on the ground."

Moses did, and the staff instantly turned into a ferocious snake. (It was so scary looking that Moses actually ran away!)

And the Lord said, "Moses, pick it up again."

I'm sure Moses wasn't excited about that, but he did as he was told. He took the snake by the tail, and it instantly turned back into a walking stick.

What was the point?

I think the Lord was telling Moses that he had everything he needed to do the job. He was saying, "You may think that's just a walking stick. But if you need it to be a trumpet, I'll turn it into a trumpet for you. If you need it to be chariot, I'll turn it into a chariot. If you need it to be a thunderous voice, great wisdom, or incredible courage, I'll turn it into those."

In other words, the Lord was saying, "Trust me. Have faith. Go and do as I've asked you. And I'll be there to help. I'll give you whatever you need to get the job done."

Remember that the Lord will be there for you too.

All right, I thought. *I'll just talk.*

And I did. I just began talking.

I must have said something funny, because everyone suddenly laughed. I remember looking down and meeting someone's eyes. And I remember thinking, "That kid is in tune with me."

And I kept talking.

I kept looking around, meeting people's eyes, and I could tell they were still with me, still listening. And I could tell I was connecting with them.

I shared an experience and read a scripture. I shared another experience, explaining what I'd learned from it, and how it had helped me. The words were just flowing, and I felt a strange sense of power like I felt in school when I was teaching my very best lesson.

And then suddenly, I was bearing my testimony. And then I was sitting down.

Many times people come up after a talk to say hi, or say thanks, or just shake my hand.

But that night I was literally mobbed by kids. And their leaders were telling me how well I'd done. And when I left I literally ran to my truck where I grabbed a pencil and paper and began writing as fast as I could, trying to remember everything I'd said.

> You might be a great leader. So one of your challenges might simply be allowing someone else to lead, to teach, or to be in charge for a change.
>
> If so, be submissive. Be happy and supportive when it's someone else's turn to be in the spotlight! Treat them the way you'd like people to treat you when you're in charge.

I'd given a couple of good talks before. (And I've given some that weren't so great.) But that night I rocked!

And I don't say that to brag, because I know it wasn't me. I was saying things I'm not smart enough to think of. I sincerely believe that the Lord magnified my ability to speak that night. He magnified my ability to express myself and to connect with those awesome young people.

And what a rush!

The whole thing was so exciting that I drove home feeling more excited and energized than I had in months. I was so grateful that in testimony meeting that Sunday I was overpowered by a need to stand and express my gratitude to my Heavenly Father.

> When the Lord gives you a task, he will prepare a way for you to get it done. (See 1 Nephi 3:7.) Remember that he not only knows a way to get it done, but he knew long before he ever gave you the job! (See 1 Nephi 9:6.)

One thing I learned is that when you're doing the Lord's work, you qualify for the Lord's help. And that he'll magnify your abilities. I learned that he'll magnify your skills, your talents, your imagination, your creativity . . .

He'll magnify whatever you need.

You gotta remember, though, that you still have to do your part. The Lord will expect you to do your best, and to do everything you can to succeed. If I had shown up at my fireside with nothing prepared, for instance, I don't think he would have been very excited to help me out.

But I had prepared.

I had practiced.

I had put in the time.

I'd written the wrong talk, yeah. But I couldn't have known that, and the Lord didn't penalize me for it.

CONSIDER FOR A SECOND A FEW OF THE CHALLENGES NEPHI FACED:

- He had to leave Jerusalem to live in the wilderness.
- He had to return to Jerusalem—a round trip of about 30 days—to get the plates of brass from Laban.
- He had to return again and convince another family (a family with several young women) to leave home and travel with them in the wilderness.
- He had to build a new bow (and arrows) to hunt with. (I once read that building a bow that actually worked was at least as difficult as building a ship.)
- He had to build a ship big and sturdy enough to carry his family across an ocean.
- He had to make plates of gold on which to engrave a record of his people.
- And then he had to actually write on those plates . . . Can you imagine how hard it must have been to scratch words into metal?
- He had to build a temple.

Have you ever noticed that Nephi's challenges became harder and harder as time went on? Almost as if the Lord was preparing him for greater and greater challenges to come?

Remember that the Lord has things in mind for you too. So when he asks you to do something simple like give a talk, do a service project, or teach a lesson, he might be preparing you for greater, more important, more challenging assignments that are weeks, months, or maybe even years down the road.

And remember that all these things will give you experience (see D&C 90:24, 122:7).

Nephi knew his scriptures pretty well. He often used Old Testament stories to motivate his older brothers. I've often wondered if he ever thought about Noah while he was working on his ship. After all, Noah had to a build a ship too. Only Noah's ship was a lot bigger than Nephi's. (It was a whole lot bigger!) Noah also had to gather up all those animals, find enough food to feed them . . . and, yeah, somebody had to clean up after the elephants!

All things considered, Nephi might have believed he was getting off pretty easy!

Now there have been times when I've been given assignments that seemed especially challenging. And the following chart's always helped me get off to a flying start. So make sure you're pencil's sharp, think of some task or chore you've got ahead of you, and give it a try. (This will be especially effective if you pick a task that seems a little overwhelming.)

Ready?

Okay . . . let's see how this goes . . .

TASK DISCOVERY!

Describe the job or assignment you need to get done:

_____

_____

_____

_____

_____

_____

Now think hard: what skills and abilities do you have that will help you get the job done?

_____

_____

_____

_____

_____

_____

What help will you need from your Heavenly Father? Don't be shy now! Make a list of everything you're going to need:

_____

_____

_____

Now be sure to ask! Be bold! Tell the Lord exactly what help you're going to need, and ask him to provide it for you. Remember Alma, who said: "[Ask] for whatsoever things ye stand in need, both spiritual and temporal" (Alma 7:23).

Now, what help will you need from other people?

_____

_____

_____

_____

_____

_____

All right . . . there are two final, super-critical steps. First, put a smile on your face. (Big smile now . . . C'mon, let's see it . . . Good job!)

And second, take action. Do something today—right now!—to get started. (Hey, I mean now! Put the book down and get to work!)

What else are you going to need? (Any special supplies, equipment, or tools?) List them here:

_____

_____

_____

Where can you get that help? Is there someone in your class or quorum you can ask? A neighbor or ward leader with special skills? Try thinking "outside the box." Remember that Nephi didn't build that ship all by himself; you shouldn't try doing everything by yourself either! Don't be afraid to get other people involved!

_____

_____

_____

Where can you get that? Again, try thinking outside the box. Do you know anyone who can help? (Do you know anyone who knows anyone?) Someone with unusual contacts or resources? Who are they?

_____

_____

_____

_____

_____

_____

Let's take an extra step here: There are a lot of people who *need* to help. People who *like* being involved. People who *need* a little attention. Can you think of anyone like that? Ask them! (Trust me . . . if you're going out of your way to help others, the Lord's really going to go out of his way to help you too.)

_____

_____

_____

_____

_____

NINE ⊙ HEY! THE MOUNTAIN'S CLOSED!
WHEN THE LORD TEACHES YOU TO FISH

"Ow, ow, ow, ow, *owwwwww*!"

Tears rolled down Wyatt's cheeks as I probed his arm. Ten years old, he was trying to be brave, but every little nudge sent bolts of pain shooting down his arm.

"Ow, ow, owwww!"

"Sorry, Wyatt," I said, trying to be as gentle as possible. "I'm being as careful as I can."

Wyatt clenched his teeth and nodded. A few minutes earlier he had caught an edge on his snowboard, flipping head-over-heels and landing hard on the snow-packed ski run. His left arm was bent at a weird angle, leaving no doubt that it was broken. I was a ski patrolman, dispatched to help him.

"Okay, kiddo," I said, satisfied that he wasn't bleeding. "I'm going to splint this . . . That'll make it feel better."

Wyatt nodded again. He clenched his eyes as I placed a splint along his arm and bandaged it in place. I was just finishing up when my friend Trevor skied up with a rescue sled.

"Hi, Trevor," I said as he stepped out of his skis. "This is Wyatt . . . He's decided to break his arm."

"Ow," Trevor said, bending down to examine the splint. "Hurts pretty bad, does it?"

"Yeah," Wyatt said.

"Oh, I hear you, brother . . . I mean, been there, done that, got the goofy T-shirt."

Wyatt laughed, the effort making him wince.

"Hey, no laughing, now," Trevor said with mock severity. "You keep that up and I'll have to make you walk down the hill."

Wyatt laughed again—wincing as he did—and I was glad it was Trevor who had come to help. He'd formed an instant bond with the injured boy, and I knew that platoons of abominable snowmen couldn't keep him from delivering Wyatt safely to the clinic at the bottom of the mountain.

We wrapped Wyatt up in the toboggan and Trevor clicked back into his skis.

"Hold on tight now, kiddo," he said, turning and pulling the sled after him, "if I can get enough speed, I'll run you through the halfpipe . . . maybe catch some air, do a flip . . ."

"Ow, ow, owwwwwwww!" Wyatt howled, laughing at Trevor's antics.

I was laughing too as Trevor skied away. I quickly packed up my gear, then glanced toward the nearest chair lift. It wasn't running. As I had worked on Wyatt, the chairlifts had shut down for the night.

Oh, great, I thought. *Now what am I gonna do?*

The problem was that I was stranded halfway down the mountain, and I still had work to do up on top. And I had no way to get there.

As I was wondering what I was going to do, I heard the growl of a snowmobile. A moment later the machine shot from the trees and turned toward me.

"Hey," I said as my friend Rob pulled up in a cloud of snow. "Am I glad to see you!"

"Yeah," Rob said, tossing me a tow rope. "The boss knew you'd be stuck so he sent me down to pick you up."

Wow, I thought as Rob towed me back up the mountain. I was grateful for the ride. And I was impressed with my boss. He'd come up with

Your Heavenly Father knows the answer to every problem you have. And he knew it before you ever had the problem!

a solution to my problem . . . before I even knew that I had a problem!

There's no place in the scriptures where someone has gone to their Heavenly Father with a problem and had him say, "Oh, wow, that's a tough one . . . I'm gonna have to call in a buncha angels and talk that one over . . ."

No, your Heavenly Father already knows the answer to every problem you have. (See 1 Nephi 9:6.) In fact, he knew the answer before you ever had the problem! And many times he'll guide you toward solutions before you even know you're in trouble.

After traveling through the wilderness for eight years, Lehi's family came to (I believe) the Indian Ocean. (See 1 Nephi 17:5.)

I would have loved to have seen the look on everyone's faces. As the family stepped over the top of the last hill and spotted that sparkling blue sea, I can just see Laman and Lemuel grinning from ear to ear. I can see them giving each other high fives and knuckle bumps, yelling "Partaaaaaaaay!" and then racing down the beach to splash in the waves.

And I can just see Nephi looking around, taking it all in, smiling to himself and thinking, *Something tells me there's another character-building experience here . . .*

And sure enough, the Lord commanded Nephi to build a ship.

Now there's an important and—I think—overlooked part of the story here. You see, Nephi needed timber to build that ship. And he needed a lot of it.

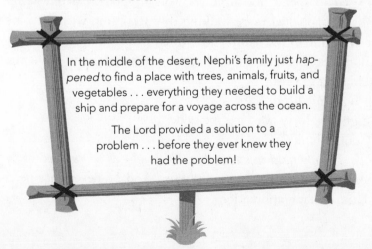

In the middle of the desert, Nephi's family just *happened* to find a place with trees, animals, fruits, and vegetables . . . everything they needed to build a ship and prepare for a voyage across the ocean.

The Lord provided a solution to a problem . . . before they ever knew they had the problem!

Not only that, but he needed animals too, not only for meat, but for skins to make bellows, tents, and clothing.

He needed ore to make tools.

He needed grain, fruit, vegetables, and a whole lotta seeds to take with him across the ocean to the promised land.

Now you've got to remember that Lehi's family had spent the last eight years in the desert. The desert! There aren't a lot of forests in the desert, and Lehi's family just happened to arrive at a place where there was plenty of timber, animals, ore . . .

Think that was a coincidence?

Neither do I!

The Lord knew what Nephi was going to need long before the family ever left Jerusalem. And as he guided them through the wilderness, he led them directly to one of the few places they'd find timber, wild animals, iron ore, fruits, vegetables, seeds . . . everything they'd need.

The Lord was providing them a solution to their problem . . . before they even knew they had a problem!

And there will be times when he'll do the same for you.

THE LORD PROVIDED LEHI'S FAMILY WITH SOLUTIONS TO THEIR PROBLEMS . . . BEFORE THEY EVEN KNEW THEY HAD THE PROBLEMS!

I used to spend my summers working at Boy Scout camp. One day I happened to be walking through camp with my boss when we came to the camp gate, which was secured with a combination lock. Ben glanced at the lock and asked, "You know the combination to this?"

I shook my head. "No."

"Eighteen, forty-two, six," he said.

"Cool. Thanks."

Like I really need to know that, I thought as we walked away. I'd been working at that camp for years. And I'd never once needed to know that combination.

That night Ben was called away from camp. So was the camp director. And the camp ranger. One of the "Big Three" was always supposed to be in camp, but that night all three of them happened to be gone.

Then, after everyone was supposed to be in bed, a bunch of mischievous Scouts began playing near their campfire. They had a little gasoline with them—which was against every rule in the universe—and they were splashing it into the fire. One of the Scouts accidently got a little gas on his bare legs . . . and then got too close to the fire.

Whoosh!

The boy's legs burst into flames. His friends got the fire out, but the boy was badly burned. He needed urgent medical attention. We needed to get him to a hospital, and we needed to get him there fast.

The only problem was that there wasn't anyone in camp who knew the combination to the gate.

Except me.

In all the years I worked at that camp, there was only one time I needed to know the combination to that gate. And the one time I needed it was the exact day I learned it. I don't think that was a coincidence. I believe with all my heart that the Lord had given me the answer to a problem . . . before I even had the problem!

There have been many times when I knew that my Heavenly Father was at work in my life, arranging things and leading me places I never would have thought of on my own. You need to know that the Lord is working behind the scenes in your life too. He has the answer to every problem you have. And—like with Nephi—he has the answer to problems that haven't even come up yet.

A word of caution, though: Even though the Lord knows the answers to your problems, there will be times he'll want you to try working things out on your own.

There's a famous quotation you might have heard, or maybe seen on a poster somewhere. "Give a man a fish and you feed him

I have students come to me all the time with math problems they don't understand. Sometimes—especially when I've got a lot going on—I feel tempted to say, "Just divide by three," or "Try the Pythagorean Theorem."

But that's not how you learn math!

As frustrating as it is sometimes, it's always better if I let the students work things out themselves, watching them as they work, nudging them in the right direction once in a while until they get it right.

I believe that the Lord often does the same thing for us. He'll often let us work out problems by ourselves, knowing that we will learn more by working through problems ourselves than by simply giving us the answers.

Be assured, though, that he'll be watching, waiting, ready to step in and help if we need it.

for a day. Teach a man to fish and you feed him for a lifetime."

Waz that mean?

It means that sometimes we learn more by working through problems ourselves than by having someone just hand us the answers.

And many times the Lord will leave problems up to us so we can learn as much as possible from the experience.

When the Lord asked Nephi and his brothers to get the plates of brass, for instance, he didn't tell them how to do it. And I think that's partly because he was "teaching them to fish." He was giving them the chance to work things out on their own. He was letting them build their confidence and—through their experience—learn about themselves.

So the brothers put their heads together and came up with a plan. I can't prove it, but I have a hunch that it was Laman's or Lemuel's idea.

Why?

Because it was so dumb!

"Hey, Laban, dude! . . . You've got these brass plates that are, like, really old and valuable, right? Well, we're on our way outta town and wondered if we could just, you know, have those . . ."

And they really thought that Laban would go for that?

They were surprised when Laban chased them off?

(As Laman walked in to talk with Laban, I can just imagine Nephi covering his face and thinking, "I am so embarrassed to be part of this . . .")

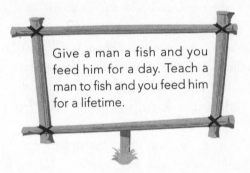

Give a man a fish and you feed him for a day. Teach a man to fish and you feed him for a lifetime.

The plan failed, of course. So the brothers tried again, this time gathering up a load of gold and silver and trying to buy the plates.

And, yeah, that didn't work either.

By now, Laman and Lemuel were ready to give up and go home. But Nephi was determined to finish the job. He snuck back into the city again. He didn't have a plan this time. But he went

As Nephi was beginning work on his ship, Laman and Lemuel came by to stir things up. They taunted their little brother, threatening to throw him off the cliff and into the sea.

But the Lord said to Nephi, "Stretch forth thine hand again unto thy brethren, and . . . I will shock them . . . that they may know that I am the Lord their God" (1 Nephi 17:13).

I love the team approach there. The Lord didn't need Nephi's help to shock the rowdy brothers. But he wanted Nephi's help. He said to Nephi, "You put your hand out, and I'll supply the shock." In other words he was saying, "You do what you can, and I'll do what you can't."

There will be times when the Lord will ask you to do your part too. And when you do everything you can, the Lord will step in to do what you can't.

anyway, knowing that as long as he was doing his part, the Lord would do his.

Remember what happened?

The Lord delivered Laban into Nephi's hands (1 Nephi 4:11).

Then Nephi—putting on Laban's clothes—went to Laban's home where he convinced Zoram (Laban's servant) that he (Nephi) was actually Laban.

Nephi doesn't come out and say so, but I think the Lord was helping out there, helping to convince Zoram that he was actually Laban. (After all, Nephi was just a kid, and Laban was an older man. And Zoram actually believed that Nephi was Laban? Hmmmm?)

I believe that was an awesome example of the Lord teaming up with someone to get the job done. As Nephi faithfully did what he could to get the plates, the Lord stepped in to make the plan work.

I mentioned that I'm a ski patrolman. I live about forty-five

When the brother of Jared built barges to cross the ocean, he realized there wouldn't be any light in them. When he reminded the Lord that it would be pretty dark inside, the Lord replied, "What will ye that I should do?" (Ether 2:23.)

In other words, the Lord was saying, "Hey, you're a pretty sharp guy . . . what ideas do you have?"

So the brother of Jared melted some rocks, creating sixteen clear stones that looked like glass. Then he went to the Lord and said, "Touch these rocks and they'll glow, giving us all the light we need."

I'm sure the Lord could have come up with a better idea than that. But I love the way he used the "team" approach. The brother of Jared did everything he could, coming up with an idea and then taking action, finding ore and smelting it to create miniature light bulbs.

And then he asked the Lord to finish the job, touching the stones so they would glow and give off light.

When you've done everything you can to solve a problem, your Heavenly Father will step in to do those things you can't!

miles away from the resort, and on snowy, stormy days it can be pretty scary getting there.

There was an especially bad storm this past winter, and I got up at 2:30 in the morning to see how bad things were. There were about eight inches of new snow on the ground, and even more was coming down.

Okay, I thought. *This isn't gonna be a whole lotta fun.*

I got dressed, fed my dog, and then knelt by my bed for a prayer. I told my Heavenly Father that I was worried about driving to Park City. I reminded him that I took my job seriously, and that I was leaving two hours earlier than usual so that I could take my time and drive as carefully as possible. And then I asked for help in making the drive safely.

The snow in Provo Canyon was deep and soft. But I drove slowly through the darkness feeling peaceful and actually enjoying the storm a little bit.

I got to Heber City okay—the halfway point—but the worst part of the drive was still ahead of me: 18 long, steep, uphill miles. I said another prayer as I drove through town toward the treacherous uphill stretch.

The road curved and I spotted a bunch of flashing yellow lights ahead.

What's this? I wondered as I drove closer. *An accident or something?*

And then—as I got closer—I realized what they were.

Snowplows!

Three, huge, extra-heavy-duty, monster snowplows!

The plows were parked along the side of the road, but as I drove closer they pulled out, forming a staggered line, and began plowing the road in front of me.

I couldn't believe it! I couldn't have timed things better if I'd called ahead and asked for a personal escort. It was almost like they'd been parked there waiting for me.

And I followed those plows all the way to Park City, driving those last harrowing miles on a clean, freshly plowed and sanded road.

Man.

Coincidence?

I don't think so. I truly believe that my Heavenly Father heard and answered my prayers. And I believe I was seeing the "team" effect in my own life. I'd done my part, leaving early enough to be able to drive slowly and carefully. And then the Lord did his, providing snowplows where I most needed them.

> In April 1829, Oliver Cowdery wanted to try translating the golden plates. When he wasn't able to, the Lord said, "Behold, you have not understood; you have supposed that I would give it unto you, when you took no thought save it was to ask me.
>
> "But, behold, I say unto you, that you must study it out in your mind; then you must ask me if it be right, and if it is right I will cause that your bosom shall burn within you; therefore, you shall feel that it is right" (D&C 9: 7–8).
>
> Notice that the Lord told Oliver that he had to do more than just ask. The Lord said, "No, you've got to first do your part. Think it over, study it out, do some research, come up with a plan. And then, Oliver, come talk to me . . . and I'll tell you if you're heading in the right direction."
>
> When you're faced with a tough problem or decision, follow that formula.
>
> Think it over.
>
> Study it out.
>
> Do some research.
>
> Ask some questions.
>
> Do your best to come up with an answer.
>
> And then—after you've done everything you can—go to your Heavenly Father. Tell him what you've done and what you've decided. And then and ask him if you've made the right decision.

You might remember how Jesus raised Lazarus from the dead (John 11). But notice how Jesus used the "team" approach: when they came to the tomb, they found it blocked by a large stone.

Jesus turned to his disciples and said, "Roll away the stone."

And then Jesus prayed, waking Lazarus, who got up and walked out of the tomb.

Jesus didn't need anyone to roll away that stone! He could have done that himself. But he was strengthening his disciples, allowing them to be part of the miracle. He was teaming up with them, saying, "Do everything that you can, and then I will do what you can't."

Now the question is, are you doing your part?

Are you "rolling away the stones" in your life before asking the Lord for help? Are you doing your best to work out your problems?

You might remember that when the Lamanite army was preparing to invade the land of Manti, Captain Moroni sent spies to follow them. (See Alma 43:22–23.)

And then Moroni sent messengers to the prophet Alma, asking him to "inquire of the Lord" where he should take his army in order to defend his people.

In the war against the Lamanites, Moroni asked his Heavenly Father for help knowing what his enemy was doing. But he still sent out spies. In other words, he asked for God's help, but then did everything he could to solve his problem.

And that's a good strategy for you too. When you need help with a problem, pray like it all depends on the Lord. But then work like it all depends on you.

When you have a problem or difficulty and the Lord is "teaching you to fish," don't give up. Don't get discouraged. Look over the following boxes for tips on tackling big problems. (Not every box will apply to every situation. But read them over and give them a try!)

Identify the Problem

Are you trying to earn an A in Killer Biology? Organize a combined activity? Reactivate a struggling friend? Be sure you know exactly what you're trying to accomplish.

Be Specific

Don't tell yourself that you need to be a better student. Instead say, "I need to get 90 percent on my next English test," or, "I need to read ten pages a day to have the whole book finished by October 15th." Be specific so you'll know exactly when you've reached your goal.

Break it Down

If you're at the bottom of a mountain looking up, it might seem like an impossible climb. So break it down into more manageable chunks. Rather than think of the entire mountain, say, "Okay . . . I've just gotta make it to the top of that first hill."

Then once you get there, set your sights on the next short-term goal.

Even if you only take five steps a day, you'll eventually get to the top!

Ask Questions

Whatever your problem or challenge is, there's someone who's been through it before.

Ask them how they did it!

Organizing a service project? Ask the person who organized the last one what *they* did.

Struggling with a science project? Find someone with an A in science and ask them for suggestions.

Success **always** leaves clues. No matter what your problem is, someone out there knows the answer . . . so **find** them! **Ask** them for ideas! Get them to help!

Release the Brakes!

You might be worried about the job ahead of you. You might think you're too young. You might think you lack the time, the skill, or the experience to succeed.

Shake off that stinkin' thinkin'!

[Or, as Lehi said, "Shake off the chains with which ye are bound" (2 Nephi 1:23).]

Get rid of whatever negative thoughts are holding you back or slowing you down!

Take a leap of faith, trust your Heavenly Father to help, and *get going*!

Don't be Afraid to Fail!

Nephi and his brothers tried and failed twice before they managed to get the brass plates.

(Nephi tried again and again and *again* to get his brothers to repent and be better . . . but that never did work out!)

If you try something that doesn't work, don't let it get you down. Tell yourself that you haven't failed, you've just found a way that doesn't work!

So don't give up! Roll up your sleeves, put a smile on your face, and **try something else!**

Take Action!

When NASA sends a rocket into space, the hardest part is just getting the thing off the ground. A rocket headed for the moon burns off most of its fuel in just the very first few minutes, and then it literally coasts the rest of the way.

You'll find that dealing with difficult problems, chores, and challenges is much the same. **The hardest part is just getting started!**

So whaddya do?

Start now!

Don't wait!

Don't put it off!

Do something today—**right now**—to break the ice and get you started!

Go the Extra Mile

When I was a missionary in Japan, my companion and I made a rule. Every time we thought it was time to stop for the day, we'd always knock on one more door. And we were amazed at how often that last door belonged to an awesome, golden family.

Think of it this way: if you heat water to 211 degrees, it's hot enough to clean the floor or wash your socks. But if you increase the temperature by one degree—just one, single degree—the water will begin to boil. It'll produce steam. And that hot water will suddenly be powerful enough to drive enormous electrical generators, mighty locomotives, and massive ships.

Imagine what you might accomplish . . . just by going the extra mile, taking that one extra step, and increasing your effort by a single degree!

Keep at it!

There's a joke about a man who tried swimming across a lake. He made it halfway, but then got so discouraged that he turned around and swam back.

Silly, isn't it?

Now whatever it is you're trying to accomplish, chances are that you're closer than you think. So don't stop. Don't give up. Like Coriantumr you might have to lean on your sword and rest once in a while (Ether 15:30), but don't ever, **ever** give up!

Take a Leap of Faith

Remember David taking on Goliath? *That* took a leap of faith.

Remember Nephi sneaking into Jerusalem, trusting the Lord to lead him? *That* was a leap of faith.

Remember Ammon standing up against a band of wicked Lamanites . . . all by himself? *That* took a leap of faith.

Whatever problem, chore, or challenge you have ahead of you, take the first step. Take that leap of faith. Like Jesus's disciples, "roll away the stone" and trust your Heavenly Father to bless your efforts.

And finally, one last idea. No matter what else you do, stay positive! Keep a good attitude! Hang in there! Joseph Smith said that "we have endured many things, and hope to be able to endure all things" (thirteenth article of faith). And the Lord has told us again and again to "endure to the end."

Remember that if the Lord is "teaching you to fish," there is something he wants you to learn from your experience. And those lessons will bless you in the future.

So look for that lesson.

Find something to learn.

Look for ways to turn your challenge into an experience that makes you even better, badder, and stronger than ever!

REMEMBER THE STORY OF DAVID AND GOLIATH?

Can you imagine this conversation taking place?

Angel: "Okay, Davey . . . that's a pretty big dude you're gonna be fighting, but we think we've got a plan."

David: "Kewl! We gonna drop a mountain on him? Zap him with a thunderbolt?"

Angel: "No, we want you to go over there and throw rocks at him."

David: "Rocks? Are you crazy? Have you seen the size of that guy? C'mon . . . let's zap him with a thunderbolt!"

Angel: "Well, the thunderbolt machine's on the fritz. So let's just give the rocks a try . . ."

David: "What if they don't work?"

Angel: "Well, how fast can you run?"

That's pretty silly, of course. But the point is that the Lord could have dropped a mountain on Goliath. He could have zapped him with a thunderbolt. There are a thousand things he could have done, saving David the trouble.

But he didn't. And he didn't offer any suggestions, either. Instead, he let David work out the problem himself, then stood by to help.

He was saying, "David, go out there and do the very best that you can. Then leave the rest to me."

The Lord's message to David is the same to you. When you're faced with a problem, go out and do your very best to solve it. And after you've done that, leave the rest up to your Heavenly Father.

TEN ⊙⊙⊙ LOST IN THE FOG
UNLEASHING YOUR INNER NEPHI

"Man, this is so cool!"

I turned my skis, braking to a stop in the soft snow. It was nearly dark, and the rugged Utah mountain was still, quiet, and cold. A thick bank of fog covered the ridges below me, looking like a huge, fluffy blanket as it stretched into the darkness.

I was working as a ski patrolman in Park City, Utah. The resort had closed for the day, and patrollers had "swept" every run on the mountain, ensuring that everyone had made it safely to the bottom.

I had remained behind as "standby," in case there were any last-minute emergencies. Being standby meant I was the last skier on the mountain. Once I reached the base, three patrollers on snowmobiles would leave summit headquarters and we'd be done for the day.

Normally there would have been another patroller to ski out with me. But tonight he'd had to help with an injury, leaving me to ski down by myself.

But that's okay, I thought as I turned my skis and whisked down the hill.

I had the whole mountain to myself!

A moment later I skied into the fog.

Cool, I thought again, loving the adventure of skiing in the fog and being all alone on the mountain.

I've got the best job in the world!

The fog was so thick it was hard to see where I was going, so I skied to my left until I could see the tall pine trees lining the run. I was feeling good, enjoying being alone on the snow.

But after a few minutes a dark shape emerged from the gloom. It took me a second to recognize it. And just like that, things weren't fun anymore.

The object was a crumbling water tower, left over from an abandoned silver mine. The problem was that it was on the wrong side of the hill.

I stopped, suddenly confused and disoriented. It took me a minute to figure it out, and when I did I felt like I had ice water pumping through my veins.

In the fog I'd missed a turn and skied down the wrong run. I was skiing into a dead-end, and the only way out was on a chair-lift, which had been closed for more than an hour.

I stood there for several minutes, trying to decide what to do. I'd skied that hill hundreds of times . . . and I couldn't believe I'd actually become lost on it.

I'm embarrassed to admit this (and I wouldn't except I feel like we've become friends), but for a couple of minutes I thought about trying to hike out. And I actually took my skis off and took about ten steps before coming to my senses.

I've already gotten lost once, I thought. *And in all this fog I might get lost again, making things even worse . . .*

I knew everyone would tease me if I called for help, but I knew there wasn't any other way. I used my cell phone (to keep everyone from hearing me), and called my boss at the summit.

And, yeah, he laughed. (I heard him telling the other snow-mobile drivers what had happened, and all three of them started howling like it was the funniest thing in the world.)

Long story short, they sent a snowmobile to get me, and I made it home safe and sound. And the next week I took a good look at the run and realized what had happened. The run I'd got-ten lost on curved gently, gradually, away from the main run. If it had been a sharp, dramatic hairpin kinda thing, I would have realized I was going the wrong way and skied back to where I belonged.

But in the fog I hadn't even realized I was turning. And I had no idea I was going the wrong way until I saw that water tower.

It was pretty embarrassing. And the scariest thing was that I didn't even know that I was lost!

I learned an important lesson that night . . . not just about skiing, but about life, and about living the gospel.

And it's a lesson I could have learned from Nephi.

Remember the story?

Lehi had a dream in which he saw crowds of people, including

Remember Peter? One stormy night he and the other disciples were on a ship when Jesus came to them, walking on the water. (Matthew 14:22–30.)

Peter (you gotta love his attitude) took one look and said, "Lord, let me come to you."

And Jesus said, "Come."

Peter hopped out of the boat and—miraculously—was able to walk on the water too.

What an awesome experience!

But then Peter took his eyes off the Lord.

He felt the strength of the wind.

He saw the blackness of the water.

And he was suddenly overcome with fear . . . and began to sink.

As long as Peter was focused on his Savior, he was able to walk on the water. The wind whipped his hair and the spray drenched his coat, but he was still safe and sound, standing atop the waves.

It was only when he took his eyes off the goal—when he looked away from the Lord—that he got into trouble.

Peter's message is the same as Lehi's: keep your eyes on the Lord. Hold tight to the iron rod. And you'll be able to withstand the mists and winds and fogs of the world.

his own family. And he saw a tree which had the most wonderful, delicious fruit in the whole world. People were trying to get to the tree, but there was a mist of darkness blocking the way. And a lot of people got lost in the mist . . . just as I did on the mountain.

But Lehi saw something else too. He saw an iron rod stretching through the fog all the way to the tree.

And those people who took hold of that rod—which Nephi explained was the word of God—didn't get lost.

They didn't get confused.

They didn't lose their way.

I've always known there was a powerful lesson there. But I never understood it as clearly as I did the night I became lost on the mountain.

Why?

Because I wanted to go the right way.

I was trying my best to go the right way.

But once I was into the fog, I didn't even realize that I was going the wrong way. (And you know what? That was the scariest part. Getting farther and farther from the right track, and not even knowing it until it was too late.)

And the lesson I learned was this: in our lives, it's easy to lose our way.

Even when we know . . . the . . . way!

And even when we trying to go the right way.

IT'S EASY TO LOSE OUR WAY IN LIFE, EVEN WHEN WE KNOW THE WAY! (AND WHEN WE'RE TRYING TO GO THE RIGHT WAY!)

But in the bumps and grinds of daily life, we can slip off the right path . . . often without realizing it. And that's why the Lord has given us that iron rod to hold on to.

Nephi explained that the iron rod was the "word of God." (See 1 Nephi 11:25, 15:24.) And that people who held on would never perish, and that the adversary would never overpower them.

Waz that mean?

In modern language, Nephi might have said that holding onto the iron rod—following the teachings of our Heavenly Father—would put us on a collision course with the Celestial Kingdom.

Nephi was so passionate about this that he pleaded with his brothers to live the commandments. He didn't just say, "Hey, guys, c'mon! It's not that tough! Swallow your pride and live a commandment every once in a while."

Nooooo!

Nephi was a lot more convincing than that. He was so passionate that he pleaded with them "with all the energies of [his] soul, and with all the faculty which [he] possessed, that they would give heed to the word of God and remember to keep his commandments always in all things" (1 Nephi 15:32).

Wow!

How would you like to hear someone speak like that at your next fireside?

But what was he saying to us?

How do we learn the word of God?

I think we can boil it down to three things.

First, **read ... your ... scriptures**.

And read them often. Read them every day. Find ways to apply them to your life. Use them to bless and improve yourself. Use them to recharge your spiritual batteries. Use them to strengthen your relationship with your Father in Heaven.

> When you read the scriptures, don't be satisfied reading a mere chapter or page a day.
>
> Instead, search for ways to strengthen your testimony.
>
> Look for ways to improve your relationship with your Heavenly Father.
>
> Look for ways to improve yourself, and to improve the quality of your life.

Second, **listen to the counsel of latter-day prophets**.

How do you do that?

Listen to general conference, and read the talks when they appear in the *Ensign*. Whatever topics the speakers choose, think of ways you can apply them to things happening in your life. Be creative. See if you can find a tip, a hint, or a suggestion you can try in every single talk.

But don't stop there! Be sure that you have a "For the Strength of Youth" pamphlet . . . and read it often. Listen closely in sacrament meeting, Sunday School, family home evening, priesthood and Relief Society meetings, and firesides for additional suggestions and counsel.

And remember this: you gotta put those ideas to work. Try to find at least one new thing you can do every day to improve yourself . . . and then do it.

If a speaker counsels you to forgive others, think of someone you're mad at and make peace!

If a speaker counsels you to keep the Sabbath holy, look for new ways to do that.

Don't think of talks as something you have to just sit and listen to. Listen for ways to lengthen your stride and quietly, consistently improve yourself.

Nephi counseled us to "liken" the scriptures to ourselves. We can do the same thing with inspirational talks. I just picked up a recent conference-talks issue of the *Ensign* and looked for ideas I could apply to my own life.

Here are the first five I came across:

1. Set a good example for others.

2. Give service.

3. Seek the power of the Holy Ghost to avoid temptations.

4. Keep myself worthy at all times.

5. Grow closer to my Heavenly Father through obedience.

Whatever topic a speaker is discussing, there are sure to be ways you can use their counsel to improve and bless yourself.

Third, **pray often**.

When it comes to offering effective prayers, Nephi set an awesome example. So if you want to improve the quality and effectiveness of your prayers, or if you want to use prayer to become closer to your Heavenly Father, do what Nephi did:

- Pray often.
- Pray boldly.
- Ponder and mediate on those things you're praying about.
- Offer thanks for the blessings you receive.
- Ask questions when you have them; ask for guidance when you need it.

Remember that our Heavenly Father wants us to succeed in this life. And that's why he's given us that rod to hold on to, to help us through the tough times.

Hold onto it!

And hold on tight!

Don't let go for anything!

In this book we've focused on Nephi, and the books he wrote. I've often thought that if First and Second Nephi were the only books we had, that we'd still have a fantastic treasure trove of tips, counsel, and lessons.

I hope you'll read them.

And I hope you'll read them again and again and again. I hope you'll look for those energizing, empowering ideas that made Nephi so excited about reading his scriptures.

President Marion G. Romney once said, "I believe with all my heart . . . that if our young people could come out of our homes thoroughly acquainted with the life of Nephi, imbued with the spirit of his courage and love of truth, they would choose the right when a choice is placed before them. How marvelous it would be if, when they must make decisions, there would flash into their minds, from long and intimate association with them, the words of Nephi: 'I will go and do the things which the Lord hath commanded'" (Conference Report, April 1960, 112).

Thanks so much for sticking this out to the last page. You're a great kid. I hope we'll meet someday, and that we can talk, and that you'll tell me some of your favorite stories.

In the meantime, get going!
Unleash your inner Nephi!
Go and do those things which the Lord has commanded!
And have an absolute blast while you're doing it!

ABOUT ⊚⊚⊚ THE AUTHOR

Shane Barker has been working with young people all his life, both as a junior high school math teacher and as the director of Boy Scout camps and high adventure bases. He has served on the faculty of National Camping School and has conducted weeklong leadership courses. An avid skier and snowboarder, Barker is an active member of the National Ski Patrol. He is a licensed pilot, a certified scuba diver, and a qualified EMT.

A popular speaker at firesides and youth conferences, Barker is the author of several books for young people. He served a mission to Japan for The Church of Jesus Christ of Latter-day Saints and later graduated from Brigham Young University. He lives in Orem, Utah.